MW00668275

HOW TO BELONG

RHETORICAND**DEMOCRATIC**DELIBERATION
VOLUME 18

EDITED BY CHERYL GLENN AND STEPHEN BROWNE
THE PENNSYLVANIA STATE UNIVERSITY

Co-founding Editor: J. Michael Hogan

Editorial Board:

Robert Asen (University of Wisconsin–Madison)
Debra Hawhee (The Pennsylvania State University)
J. Michael Hogan (The Pennsylvania State University)
Peter Levine (Tufts University)
Steven J. Mailloux (University of California, Irvine)
Krista Ratcliffe (Marquette University)
Karen Tracy (University of Colorado, Boulder)
Kirt Wilson (The Pennsylvania State University)
David Zarefsky (Northwestern University)

Rhetoric and Democratic Deliberation focuses on the interplay of public discourse, politics, and democratic action. Engaging with diverse theoretical, cultural, and critical perspectives, books published in this series offer fresh perspectives on rhetoric as it relates to education, social movements, and governments throughout the world.

A complete list of books in this series is located at the back of this volume.

HOW TO BELONG

WOMEN'S AGENCY IN A TRANSNATIONAL WORLD

BELINDA STILLION SOUTHARD

The Pennsylvania State University Press | University Park, Pennsylvania

Library of Congress Cataloging-in-Publication Data

Names: Stillion Southard, Belinda A., 1978– author.
Title: How to belong : women's agency in a transnational
world / Belinda Stillion Southard.
Other titles: Rhetoric and democratic deliberation.
Description: University Park, Pennsylvania : The
Pennsylvania State University Press, [2018] | Series:
Rhetoric and democratic deliberation | Includes
bibliographical references and index.
Summary: "Explores the question of how women craft
meaningful 'belonging' to national, regional, and global
communities when belonging as a citizen becomes
untenable. Evaluates the rhetorical practices that
enable alternative belongings, such as denizenship,
cosmopolitan nationalism, and transnational
connectivity"—Provided by publisher.
Identifiers: LCCN 2018026213 | ISBN 9780271082004
(cloth : alk. paper) | ISBN 9780271082011 (pbk : alk.
paper)
Subjects: LCSH: Women civic leaders. | Rhetoric—
Political aspects. | Belonging (Social psychology) |
Transnationalism.
Classification: LCC HQ1390.S75 2018 | DDC 305.8—dc23
LC record available at https://lccn.loc.gov/2018026213

Chapter 2 is revised from "Crafting Cosmopolitan
Nationalism: Ellen Johnson Sirleaf's Rhetorical
Leadership," by Belinda Stillion Southard,
published in *Quarterly Journal of Speech*. © National
Communication Association reprinted by permission
of Taylor & Francis Ltd, http://www.tandfonline.com,
on behalf of National Communication Association.

Copyright © 2018 Belinda Stillion Southard
All rights reserved
Printed in the United States of America
Published by The Pennsylvania State University Press,
University Park, PA 16802–1003

The Pennsylvania State University Press is a member
of the Association of University Presses.

It is the policy of The Pennsylvania State University
Press to use acid-free paper. Publications on uncoated
stock satisfy the minimum requirements of American
National Standard for Information Sciences—
Permanence of Paper for Printed Library Material,
ANSI Z39.48–1992.

To Bjørn, Ella, & Finna

CONTENTS

ABBREVIATIONS

AWDF	African Women Development Fund
CSW	Commission on the Status of Women
ECOWAS	Economic Community of West African States
IGO	intergovernmental organization
LWI	Liberian Women's Initiative
LWP	African Women and Peace Support Group, *Liberian Women Peacemakers: Fighting for the Right to Be Seen, Heard, and Counted* (Trenton: Africa World Press, 2004)
MARWOPNET	Mano River Women of Peace Network
MBOP	Leymah Gbowee and Carol Mithers, *Mighty Be Our Powers: How Sisterhood, Prayer, and Sex Changed a Nation at War* (New York: Beast Books, 2011)
MRU	Mano River Union
NGO	nongovernmental organization
RUF	Revolutionary United Front
SMWF	Sirleaf Market Women's Fund
TCWBG	Ellen Johnson Sirleaf, *This Child Will Be Great: Memoir of a Remarkable Life by Africa's First Woman President* (New York: HarperCollins, 2009)
UN	United Nations
UNSCR	United Nations Security Council Resolution
WIPNET	Women in Peace Network

ACKNOWLEDGMENTS

All of the following people have generated a community of care, a community that posed the necessary challenges, asked the necessary questions, and practiced the care and curiosity to make this book. So, to:

Kendra Boileau, Alex Vose, Brian Beer, Regina Starace, and the rest of the Penn State University Press team, who made this publication process an absolute delight. Two anonymous reviewers whose investment in this manuscript not only made it smarter and sharper, but also showed care for the vitality of the discipline that I will pay forward. Barbara Biesecker's support of my early career at University of Georgia, which included nominating me for a UGA Summer Research Grant, which supported the initial stages of this book's research. Graduate students Jason Williamson, Anna Dudney Deeb, and Hillary Palmer, whose dedicated and tedious research supported this project's nascent stages. Kari Anderson for her brilliant response at Texas A&M's Civic Dialogue and Leadership conference and her feminist collegiality. Seminarians from RSA's 2015 seminar on Citizenship and Rhetoric, especially Ersula Ore and Damien Pfister. The seminar's leaders, Cate Palczewski and Karma Chávez, for inviting me to join the group and who engaged the project. Leslie Pace at University of Louisiana at Monroe, Tim Barney at University of Richmond, and Sally Spalding at Southeast Missouri State University for hosting me at their campuses and facilitating guest lectures on the book's research. Leslie, Tim, and Sally for taking time to generate the connection and kindness that academics often don't or can't make the time to do. My spring 2016 graduate seminarians in Transnational Rhetorical Studies who joined me on this research journey. You were curious, bold, and whip smart. Barbara Biesecker for inspiring chapter 2's focus on cosmopolitanism. Bradford Vivian and two anonymous reviewers for guiding the chapter's earlier version into publication at *Quarterly Journal of Speech*. Tarez Samra Graben and Rebecca Richards for including and engaging me on their panel at ISHR. Audience members of all the conference presentations, invited talks, and colloquia who listened, considered, and asked questions.

Clint Graves for an exquisite index. My colleagues at UGA for friendship and mentorship. Sally Spalding for her excellent copyediting, child care, self-invitations for dinner, mental health care, and kindness. Lisa Corrigan for her radical friendship. Bjørn Stillion Southard as a joyful companion in work, parenting, and life.

INTRODUCTION:
RHETORICS OF BELONGING
IN A TRANSNATIONAL WORLD

In 1995, five years into Liberia's first civil war, Theresa Leigh-Sherman, Evelyn Townsend, and Clara d'Almeida set off to Abuja, Nigeria, determined to speak at a peace conference. Leigh-Sherman, Townsend, and d'Almeida learned that if they wanted to be heard, they had to demand attention at these male-dominated meetings. In the previous year, a coalition of women's groups raised funds to send a delegation of women to a conference sponsored by the Economic Community of West African States (ECOWAS) in Accra, Ghana. When the women asked for invitations, ECOWAS leaders thought the women were joking and declined to invite them. However, after raising enough money to purchase six conference tickets, the women were allowed to attend. Upon their arrival, they found that they could not participate in the conference—that they couldn't even sit in the same room as the men. So they sat outside of the room and waited until the men took breaks. During which, the women lobbied faction leaders and ECOWAS representatives for a part in the peace talks. After three days of lobbying, the women were finally granted "participant status," which allowed them to listen—but not speak—to the men in the meeting.

Despite their many obstacles, Leigh-Sherman, Townsend, and d'Almeida would not settle for "participant status." Leigh-Sherman recalls the challenges they faced: "We were so bad off financially, we hardly had clothes, I mean we had nothing except will power. We were proud to be Liberians, and we felt it was time for the international community to hear our side of the story."[1] To tell their side of the story, the women began pressuring ECOWAS officials as soon as they arrived in Abuja. Most told them, "The program is set; you're not on the agenda" (*LWP*, 26). But upon delivering his opening remarks, the ECOWAS president spontaneously called Leigh-Sherman to the stage because, as he put it, "We have never listened to the civilians, we have never listened to our mothers, we have never listened to our sisters" (26). Leigh-Sherman remembers how she and the other two women responded: "We just grabbed each other's hands, we were shaking because it looked [like] God had heard our prayers. . . . We talked about the killing and how these men were opening these women's stomachs and betting on the babies. We talked about everything because the women were tired. We were just tired. . . . And I tell you the nine Presidents that were there . . . [were] in tears because these are facts that these people didn't know about. . . . But we had gone through it. We had lost everything we worked for" (26). Their participation in Abuja represented a turning point for women in the peacemaking process. From that point forward, ECOWAS actively recruited women leaders to bring warring factions together for peace talks (27).

If we think about this anecdote from a rhetorical perspective, we can appreciate the ways in which women like Leigh-Sherman, Townsend, and d'Almeida asserted rhetorical agency. They were constrained by many factors, including experiences of sexual assault, displacement, the murder of family members and destruction of their villages, lack of money and resources, lack of recognition as political actors, and their responsibilities as mothers to protect their children. They were also enabled by other factors, including a coalition of women's organizations, donors willing to fund their travel, the experiences of the women in Accra, a unique knowledge of wartime atrocities, the "will power" to stop violence, and their positions as "mothers" and "sisters." From a rhetorical perspective, we might say that from within the constraints and possibilities of their rhetorical situation, these women persuaded their audiences to listen to them.

However, if we situate this rhetorical situation in a transnational feminist context, we can see that the women's rhetoric negotiated much more than their audience's resistance to listening. First, they negotiated national and regional affiliations. While they identified as proud Liberians working for peace in Liberia, they also engaged regional women's organizations and regional governing bodies for money and support. Moreover, they crossed national (and factional) lines in order to travel throughout West Africa. Likewise, the meetings they attended were led by ECOWAS, one of eight regional economic communities that make up the African Union. Second, these women negotiated the gendered boundaries of peacemaking politics. At this point, many women's organizations had successfully negotiated with factional leaders to ensure the safe delivery of food and health care to victims of war but had not yet earned a seat at the negotiation table. They believed that their wartime experiences *as women*, as mothers of the children lost, conscripted, and murdered, positioned them as ideal participants. They possessed knowledge that political elites "didn't know about." They came to share their concrete, lived experiences of displacement, murder, and losing "everything" that transcended their village, ethnic, religious, and national identifications such that the women were united in one way: the "women were tired." Recognized as civilians, mothers, and sisters, they were finally allowed to speak.

Considering how these women negotiated geographic and gendered boundaries foregrounds the ways in which their rhetoric negotiated what it meant to belong. Because soldiers had treated their bodies like factional and national property, these women had experienced what it meant for a nation and its warring factions to violently exclude populations that don't belong. Because these women and their children had been displaced and their villages had been burned to the ground, their search for safer places eroded their sense of belonging to a family and to a home. Forging networks across factional and national lines enabled them to find belonging with women from Sierra Leone and Guinea, women who identified themselves by their national belonging ("proud to be Liberians") *as well as* their regional belonging (as women of West Africa appealing to a West African organization). Through their rhetorical practices, these women articulated belonging as relationships with other women that simultaneously recognized and superseded their belonging as national citizens. These relationships, I find, enabled these women to reimagine how to belong in a transnational world.

How these West African women and women elsewhere in the world reimagined belonging is the central concern of this book. The following section unpacks how I arrived at "belonging" as a rhetoric that foregrounds relationships between women that enable them to engage and challenge nationalist discourses of belonging. Moreover, this introduction situates citizenship, rhetorical agency, and transnational feminist rhetoric as key analytics for understanding how I read "rhetorics of belonging."

Belonging, Rhetoric, and National Citizenship

With the rise of globalization, transnational flows of political and economic power have thrown into question the power of the nation-state. Scholars observe that as the boundaries of nation-states yield to the power of multinational corporations, regional economic unions, and the norms of global governing bodies, they become increasingly porous and flexible. In turn, goods, resources, and people move with increasing speed and intensity around the globe.[2] At the same time, nation-states have worked to reestablish the rigidity of their boundaries, intensifying their power to define who belongs and who does not to a national community.[3] Contrary to claims that we might live in a postnational society, the world has seen more restrictive immigration and refugee laws, regional skirmishes and turf wars, and at least in the United States, heightened concerns and resources for "national security"—all of which point to the power of the state apparatus to shape what belonging means in concrete ways.[4] The simultaneous porousness and rigidity of national boundaries has resulted in heightened global crises, such as human trafficking, starvation, extreme poverty, bloody conflict, and most central to this project, the extraordinary abuse of women and girls.[5] It is estimated that 60 percent of the world's hungry are women, 70 percent of women worldwide have experienced some form of sexual violence, and women comprise two-thirds of the world's illiterate population.[6] Correspondingly, the world has seen a rise of transnational and regional grassroots movements, supranational attention and resources distributed to poor nations and regions, and the development of global norms of human rights to be taken up by nation-states.[7] Thus, the increasing transnationalization of the world has brought into sharp focus the empowering and disempowering contours of national boundaries.

As national boundaries flex and retract in response to the forces of nationalism, global capitalism, regionalism, and global governance, scholars have revisited what and how much it means to belong to a national community. If national boundaries are increasingly flexible and fluid, how important is belonging to a national community compared to regional or global communities, or to cultural, religious, and/or ethnic communities?[8] Likewise, if national boundaries are increasingly rigid and exclusionary, especially in terms of the nation-state's power to define who has access to certain rights and privileges that for many can mean life or death, how can national belonging *not* matter the most to inhabitants of this world? Is it possible to belong to national, regional, and global communities all at once, or to move in and out of belonging in strategic ways? And if so, what does this movement look like? In rhetorical terms, *how* do rhetors express and craft belonging to negotiate the empowering and disempowering forces at play in a globalized world of asymmetrical power flows?

Resoundingly, scholars have answered these questions by reimagining belonging as expanded or reconfigured meanings of *citizenship*. Studies from geography, international relations, political science, anthropology, women's studies, and rhetorical studies have offered concepts such as global citizenship, corporate citizenship, cosmopolitan citizenship, and cultural citizenship to explain current challenges to national citizenship.[9] In his study of global community, Robert DeChaine's research query is illuminating: "Given the shifting nature of the relationships between local, national, and global 'loyalties[,]' . . . what form(s) of *citizenship* will dominate in a globalized world?"[10] Centering on citizenship makes sense because historically, the idea of belonging to a defined place—a place with boundaries both real and imagined—can be traced back to Greco-Roman ideals of belonging as citizenship. Classically construed, citizenship to a city-state was defined by the ability to speak before and be recognized by one's community. No doubt, this ability was and continues to be granted to an exclusive group. Nonetheless, to belong to a city-state meant to practice rhetoric, and to practice rhetoric meant that one could shape the city-state.[11] In terms of the modern democratic state, if one is recognized as a citizen, then one is likely able to address one's community in ways that officially "count": for example, voting, petitioning, speaking in town halls, writing for editorial columns. Similarly, being able to access education, health care, and tax breaks allows one to imagine, as Benedict Anderson posited, that one belongs to an educated, healthy, and equitable community of national citizens.[12]

That said, it is no secret that the ideals and the realities of citizenship belonging can diverge, and quite radically so. A robust body of scholarship examines national citizenship for how it works as a rhetorically shaped and contested construct, as an enabling and (violently) disabling category, and as an ideologically and historically fraught ideal.[13] Many rhetorical studies expose how political elites crafted arguments in favor of or against citizenship rights—arguments shaped in part by their constituents' demands for enhanced or restricted citizenship rights.[14] Studies also demonstrate how those excluded from the national community, legally and otherwise, have rhetorically challenged the laws and social norms of exclusion toward inclusion and more so, toward revised ideals.[15] Some studies debunk citizenship altogether because of the violent exclusions that accompany nationalist projects to define membership.[16] That said, studies of extremely violent protests against the nation-state argue that protest groups engage in violence in part because they recognize that the state apparatus possesses remarkable legal and rhetorical power to define who belongs and how.[17]

Because of the historical and complicated relationship between rhetoric and citizenship, as practices and as ideals, it's no wonder that when attempting to explain belonging in light of recent challenges to the power of the nation-state, scholars have done so in terms of citizenship. My intervention into these conversations seeks to account for how globalization has provoked reimaginings of belonging to relationships and places in ways that decenter national citizenship. Consider, for example, that over the last two decades, we have witnessed the regional mobilization of women antiwar protesters bring an end to years of bloody conflicts in West African nations. Likewise, among democratic nations, we've witnessed a sharp uptick in the direct election of women presidents—the most difficult way for a woman to access the presidency—who are explicitly committed to mainstreaming women's rights in their nations and across the globe. Further, the world has seen the organization of global governing bodies primarily dedicated to empowering women and girls worldwide. These phenomena suggest that as membership in the nation-state has become increasingly tenuous and contentious, women have reimagined belonging in ways that have enabled them to negotiate belonging to regional, national, and global communities and, in the process, to redefine belonging to a transnational world in kinder, more favorable ways.

In this book, I examine how women leaders around the world crafted belonging to communities in ways that engaged and pushed back against national citizenship as the primary form of belonging. In so doing, I attend to the upshot of transnational flows of power—for how these flows forged pathways for rhetorical leaders to craft belonging as relationships among women who are situated as ideal constituents of a place, real and imagined. Specifically, I examine how women's rhetoric crafted belonging as regional denizenship, national cosmopolitanism, and transnational connectivity. These types of belonging do not replace or discount national citizenship. Rather, they are held in relationship to national citizenship such that it is recontextualized as part and parcel to these types of belonging. This recontextualization, then, put women in relationship to one another as denizens, cosmopolitans, and connectors, which in turn allowed them to access political power and assert rhetorical agency as constituents of regions, nations, and the world. Belonging to these relationships and places enabled women to engage the nation-state as active participants in crafting what it means to belong to their communities.

To the women under study in this book—grassroots protesters, a president, and a UN director—belonging is not simply a legal status defined by a state apparatus; it is a relationship between women imagined as the ideal constituents of a region, a nation, and the world. These women asserted rhetorical agency from within contexts shaped by economic, social, and political ideologies and institutions historically and materially unkind to women. As they negotiated multiple agentic forces at play in an increasingly transnational context, they enacted and promoted concrete rhetorical practices that worked to reshape belonging for the disenfranchised women and girls of their communities. The following section explicates the motivation for this study as part of our responsibility as critics to locate the conditions of possibility and the rhetorical practices at work to reimagine belonging in empowering ways.

Belonging, Citizenship, and Rhetorical Agency

The heart of this project asks after rhetorical agency. What constitutes rhetorical agency? Why has belonging been so intimately tied to rhetorical agency and, more pointedly, tied to agency as national citizens? When examining the power of rhetoric in a transnational context, where is agency located, and what implications does this have on the extent to which women can assert themselves as rhetors? Finally, what is the relationship between rhetorical agency and rhetorical practice? The following examines the relationships between these terms, especially in the ways that scholars of rhetoric and composition and public address have discussed them. From within these scholarly conversations, I situate rhetorical agency as the conditions of possibility and assertion of rhetorical practices constitutive of belonging.

Agency can be explained as one's can-do-ness. Rhetorical agency, broadly construed, attends to what enables one to do rhetoric and how, where, and when one can do rhetoric. Put another way by Kenneth Burke, if rhetoric is "equipment for living," then rhetorical agency is the ability to access and use the equipment.[18] The dominant conceptualization of rhetorical agency in the ancient world, shaped by Aristotle and Isocrates, supposed that an agent, an educated and recognized member of the city-state, assessed their situation and audience in order to craft the most effective rhetorical strategies. Throughout the centuries, emphases on a privileged "good man speaking well" via a strategic combination of invention, delivery, arrangement, memory, and style cemented a view of a singular actor whose speech act would favorably alter their circumstances.[19] In the twentieth century, Burke's theorizing helped destabilize and expand on these assumptions. He argued that rhetorical agency is located in "acting-together" to create "common sensations, concepts, images, ideas, attitudes."[20] To Burke, the desire to communicate stemmed from a dialectical relationship between identification and division with "men," an ongoing negotiation and struggle to consubstantiate and, in turn, make and use the equipment necessary for living. Thus, rhetorical agency was always already at play.

As many feminist rhetoricians have noted, Burke may have pushed the idea of rhetorical agency away from singular notions of situation, speaker, and speech, but he did very little to recognize the privilege of the who, what, and where of rhetorical agency.[21] Hallmark works such as Karlyn Kohrs Campbell's two-volume *Man Cannot Speak for Her*, Cheryl Glenn's *Rhetoric Retold*, and Shirley Wilson Logan's *With Pen and Voice* and *"We Are Coming"* illustrated that historically, women did (and can) assert rhetorical agency as persuasion over a particular audience. These works also provoked a retheorization of rhetorical agency to account for women's subjectivities and the form and content of their discourse.[22] Correspondingly, feminist theorists sought to recognize women's knowledges, standpoints, and rhetorical aptitudes as situated, multiple, and negotiated.[23] Further, the rise of poststructural feminist theories held that because discourse always already constrains an agent's ability to generate discourse, then rhetorical agency lies as much in the agent as it does in the discourses that enable and constrain them.[24]

To varying degrees, rhetorical critics have taken up these theories, examining rhetorical agency in and across a number of forces, including speakers; texts; contexts; texts-in-contexts; political, economic, social, cultural, temporal, and/or ideological constraints; institutions; communities; technologies; and so on. Bonnie J. Dow observes that most studies of women rhetors attribute rhetorical agency to rhetors, rhetorical acts, and contextual forces. These studies work to appreciate rhetors whose subject positions likely limited their rhetorical choices and effects.[25] At the same time, these projects seek to critique the historically and ideologically inflected contexts that created the conditions of their exclusion in the first place.[26] Campbell argues that rhetorical agency is "the capacity to act, that is, to have the competence to speak or write in a way that will be recognized or heeded by others."[27] Noting the gendered limits of this model, she acknowledges that rhetors are more than individuals who make strategic choices. She adds, "Rhetors/authors, because they are linked to cultures and collectivities, must negotiate among institutional powers and are best described as 'points of articulation' rather than originators."[28] Echoing Michael Calvin McGee's theory of constitutive rhetoric, Campbell argues that rhetors and their rhetorics are called into being by their community's discourse, which enables rhetors to assert rhetorical agency as members of their community.[29]

In tandem, rhetorical criticism over the last few decades has located rhetorical agency in texts, most often treated as something in between a hermeneutically sealed product and as a series of "fragments" connected over periods of time.[30] Speaking to a "middle way" between Michael Leff's close textual methodology and McGee's fragmentation thesis, John Angus Campbell presciently avers that criticism could hold "the local stability of a text in its context" in "dynamic equilibrium" with "the local stability of an ideology changing gradually over time."[31] Indeed, over the last two and a half decades, rhetorical critics have analyzed the rhetorical agency of texts as highly situated rhetorical practice that shape and are shaped by historically entrenched yet dynamic ideologies.

Belonging, Rhetorical Agency, and Transnational Feminist Rhetoric

So how do rhetoricians treat rhetorical agency in a transnational world? Over the last two decades, a handful of studies have attributed rhetorical agency to global forces and bodies, and to ideologies, norms, and institutions with influence beyond that of the nation-state. Some are skeptical about the power of rhetorical actors to influence or challenge the interconnected forces of organizations such as the International Monetary Fund and the World Health Organization, of the contradictory ideals of economic liberalism and political liberalism,[32] and of the "megarhetorics" of global development.[33] These studies find that through discourses such as presidential rhetoric, social responsibility campaigns, group protests, and documentary films, individuals (specifically presidents) and groups can engage and resist the disempowering forces of globalization. Most of this scholarship, however, starts with the assumption that globalization, development, and neoliberal policies significantly decrease the potential for rhetorical actors to engage and respond. Moreover, they expose how these dominant forces work rhetorically and how rhetorical efforts to counteract these forces, to an extent, bend to dominant vectors of power.[34]

The most nuanced and robust studies of rhetoric, transnationalism, and agency come from transnational feminist rhetorical studies. In the early 1990s, transnational feminism emerged as a critical framework and an activist project that seeks to exploit the increasingly fluid boundaries of the nation-state in order to destabilize and rewrite boundaries of belonging.[35] Like rhetorical studies of globalization, transnational feminist studies often focus on how neoliberal political economies affect women and girls. Some emphasize the potential for women to reimagine and transform their national, regional, and hemispheric belongings in order to create alliances and coalitions and, in turn, to assert collective agency to blunt global flows of power.[36] These transformations can offer points of entry into global structures where women can assert themselves as political actors to help undo globalization's material consequences, such as poverty, starvation, sexual assault, and human trafficking.[37] Feminist critics are compelled to account for how rhetorics travel between and among local, global, national, and supranational communities, as well as to unpack how this circulation creates what Inderpal Grewal popularly terms "transnational connectivities," which shape symbolic and material realities for women.[38]

Rhetorical agency, especially in a transnational context, cannot be fully possessed nor controlled, for its force is dispersed, networked, and interconnected. Moreover, it cannot be traced back to any one particular person, thing, context, or moment because it flows, traffics, and moves in unpredictable ways. The job of the rhetorical critic of transnationalism and its attendant forces, then, is to unpack how, where, and when transnationalism is expressed through symbols and practices, and how these symbols and practices intensify meanings that enable and reshape symbolic and material realities toward a more empowered and/or disempowered humanity.

Given this understanding of rhetorical agency, however, I wonder whether, as rhetorical critics, we've focused so much on the movements of transnational discourses at the cost of overlooking the practices that mediate and galvanize its movements. Foregrounding how discourses network and move backgrounds significant parts of the rhetorical equation: the rhetorical practices, the "acting-together," and the communicative nodes that propel, amplify, and/or ricochet the movement of discourse. I realize these foci are the result of different research questions and emphases. Bringing rhetorical practices into sharp relief is in part motivated by the fact that transnational feminist theory seeks to understand not only how multiple agentic forces have enabled and constrained women but also how women, in concrete ways, can and have asserted agency. Sociologist, Myra Marx Ferree, for example, recently observed: "Despite the typical assumption that globalization is a massive force bearing down on helpless populations, to look at the actual process is to see a great variety of social actors—including many who are not educational or political elites—engaging in diverse types of integrative work."[39] Likewise, Peggy Levitt argues that we need to resist "transnational determinism," a perspective in which "actors tend to be depicted as heavily constrained, with little agency."[40] Thus, a transnational feminist analysis, according to Marcia Texler Segal and Esther Ngan-ling Chow, should not only expose how transnationalism positions women within asymmetrical power relationships, both locally and globally, but also how it "enables us to see women as change agents . . . to form transnational alliances and to engage in the politics of transnational feminist praxis across national boundaries."[41]

An examination of how women have engaged in "transnational feminist praxis" compels an analysis of how women have done so through *rhetorical* practice. Rhetoricians are especially suited to this task, especially if we take as our critical purpose to expose how symbols shape and are shaped by realities with particular focus on building a more empowered humanity. To these ends, it's necessary to expand on transnational feminist theory to account for women's rhetorical acts and, in turn, their meaning-making possibilities.

Rhetorical Practices in Transnational Feminist Studies:
Focus and Method

Undoubtedly, transnational feminist rhetorical studies are concerned with women's rhetorical agency, though they answer different questions about the location and force of agency. Most recently, Rebecca Dingo's *Networking Arguments* exposes how rhetorics travel and take different shapes through supranational and national women's rights policy discourses.[42] In turn, Dingo pointedly identifies how these discourses materialized certain realities for women. In her study, then, the agents weren't individual rhetors per se, but policymakers at work in supranational and national decision-making bodies. Rebecca S. Richards's *Transnational Feminist Rhetorics* focuses on discourses that constituted "women world leaders" both as embodied agents and as a constraining and enabling ideology.[43] Though her arguments relied on some rhetorical acts of the leaders themselves, the book mostly examined discourses created about these leaders and how those discourses interrupted and generated expectations for women leaders worldwide.[44] Richards's project brought much-needed attention to the discourses that are mapped onto women world leaders and how we need a more complex way of understanding the rhetorical force of women world leaders as a growing entity of human beings and as a globally shared construct.

This book focuses on the rhetorical practices of women leaders. Like Richards, I'm careful not to view women leaders as individuals with unmitigated power to persuade others. Instead, I view them as embodied subjects, enabled and constrained by the flows and ebbs of transnational currents, and most importantly for this study, as agents of rhetorical practice. I share

Jacqueline Jones Royster and Gesa E. Kirsch's recent assessment of rhetorical agency as "an embodied social praxis that enacts itself variously across cultures and around the globe."[45] Viewing rhetorical practices as embodied acts or as enactments of "social praxis," rhetorical agency in transnational contexts pushes back against "leader-centered rhetorical criticism" and resists the totalizing practice of ascribing change to the "lone hero" rhetor.[46] In my view, Arabella Lyon's recent book *Deliberative Acts* best demonstrates how critics can account for how concrete and situated rhetorical acts shape transnational rhetorics and vice versa. Arguing that rhetorical agency must account for "the materiality of situated agents' bodies," Lyon examines how Eman al-Obeidi, a Libyan lawyer, staged her testimony on being raped and tortured by speaking to international journalists in the lobby of a Western hotel, which in turn elicited a worldwide social media campaign for her freedom.[47] Lyon's close textual analysis of al-Obeidi's words, actions, and their effects provokes more analyses of how women assert rhetorical agency in concrete ways and in her words, "with care."[48]

I aim to bring into focus women's "rhetorical acts" in the study of rhetorical agency and their role in transnational meaning-making "with care." First, I acknowledge that as a First World white cisgender woman, trained and educated in Western institutions, I cannot relate to grassroots peace movement leaders, presidents of war-torn nations, and UN directors. Nor can I fully relate to their situations, their realities, their constraints. My job as a rhetorical critic, as I see it, is to offer an account of women's rhetoric with as much richness and depth as possible, while remaining as fully aware of my situated and privileged perspective as possible. I take up what LuMing Mao considered the "ultimate form of rhetorical responsibility": to consider and bring to the reader the multiple contexts in which rhetorics emerge, including epistemological, ethical, and political contexts.[49] This is to say that when studying rhetors whose rhetorical practices, to different extents, are crafted from within and beyond the androcentric Greco-Roman tradition, the critic must situate texts within multilayered contexts—contexts shaped by local, national, regional, and global vectors of power. Just as important, I believe, is to track how, from within and between multiple agentic forces, these texts transformed oppressive and singular modes of belonging into multiple and favorable modes of belonging. These women and their discourses are complex and nuanced and thus deserve care and empathy. Realizing that I arrive at their discourses in partial and privileged ways, I aim to practice care and empathy through rigorous contextualization prior to evaluating the force of their rhetorical practices. As Angela Ray put it, understanding people as "living in their times" gives us the best chance to examine how rhetoric works within its rhetorical context.

Second, my focus on rhetorical practice serves to catalogue particular strategies that may in fact be replicated, adopted, appropriated, adjusted, rearticulated, and/or downright rejected—but at the very least considered—toward a greater project of empowering women. This hope assumes that, to an extent, rhetorical practices are concrete things that can be taken up and recontextualized, emulated, and practiced in new ways. That said, my understanding of rhetorical agency resists a view of rhetorical practice as something *absolutely* concrete. I see these practices as snapshots or bracketed moments along a time line, but the brackets hang precariously, and no one knows when the time line began, how long or far it will travel, or if it's not a line at all but instead one vector of many in a three-dimensional discursive field. Lyon offers us another way to think about these moments. Drawing on Hannah Arendt, she calls scholars to consider communication as the in-between-ness of all of those gathered around the table, to "focus not on agent or act, but the shared potential of those at the table."[50] As such, she continues, "Any act within an in-between is not easily owned or attributed."[51] Thus, this book views the rhetorical practices of women leaders as in-between asser-tions of rhetorical agency that express both conditions of possibility and the materialization of one's potential to act. Specifically, the rhetorical practices I examine are treated as the in-between, the nodes, and connectivities along the diffuse, networked, and flowing movements of transnational feminist rhetorics. Rhetorical practices both reflect and shape the transnational world in which they hold currency. It is with this sense of local and temporary sta-bility that I examine women's rhetorical practices as fugacious expressions of rhetorical agency.

Rhetorics of Belonging

As discussed previously, the relationship between rhetoric and citizenship is an ideologically and historically fraught one. Often nation-states define citi-zenship in terms of the types of things citizens can or cannot do or in terms of how nation-states create or restrict the conditions necessary for a citizen to assert rhetorical agency. Robert Asen highlights how scholars have too often focused on the "what" of citizenship, a question or mode that lends itself to legally prescribed definitions of belonging to the nation-state. Asking the "how" of citizenship is a question that lends itself to viewing citizenship as practice, performance, and mode of engagement.[52] Put plainly by Danielle Allen, "Ordinary habits are the stuff of citizenship."[53] This emphasis on the everyday and ordinary corroborates with a constitutive view of rhetoric, which holds that performing certain acts can constitute the self as a citizen in ways recognized by the nation-state or not. This view suggests that one's subject position is not fully determined by the labels and categories imposed by a state apparatus. In fact, Richard Marback highlights the rhetorical agency of the self to craft one's subjectivity: "What people do matters more for their understandings of themselves as citizens than the descriptions of citizenship given them by law."[54] That said, I wonder: What if discourses, legal, cultural, social, and otherwise, constrained people's ability to see their actions as expressions of *citizenship* per se? In light of overwhelming evidence that, worldwide, women and girls have been physically and symbolically shoved to the edges, the limits, the corners of what counts as *citizenship*, how can they act or speak in ways heeded by their communities? What if their capacity "to be heard" *as citizens* by their communities, in ways constituted through their everyday acts and/or through cultural, social, and/or legal norms—offered so few rhetorical resources to assert agency as rhetorical actors that they reimagined belonging to their communities within and perhaps beyond the discourses of citizenship? This book explores what happens when rhetorical practices enact belonging through relationships in addition to and apart from those tied to the nation-state and citizenship. The following elaborates on how scholars can study *belonging* as a rhetoric of relations to places, real and imagined. In order for critics to examine the possibilities of belonging as something articulated to or dislodged from national citizenship, it's important to examine the emancipatory limits and possibilities of assertions of belonging.[55]

In 2005, Aimee Carrillo Rowe theorized belonging as a *politics of relation*, an alternative to a *politics of location*. Rather than thinking of belonging as the way an individual relates to a particular place (as in one's subjectivity and/or one's geographic location), she instead "gestures toward deep reflection about the selves we are creating as a function of where we place our bodies, and with whom we build our affective ties."[56] Rowe argues that our subject positions are effects of our desire to belong, to be "radically inclined toward others, toward the communities to which we belong, with whom we long to be, and to whom we feel accountable."[57] Rowe puts forth the notion of "differential belonging" as "inclusion as a vehicle to move."[58] This movement, as taken up by Karma R. Chávez, can help forge coalitions across groups in ways that shift "the locus of belonging" away from state-sanctioned citizenship. "This alternative locus," she continues, "provides a rationale for all people oppressed by capitalism to long to be in relation to one another."[59] To Rowe and Chávez, then, rhetorical agency is not necessarily a force that originates within the individual. Resonating with transnational feminist theory, when people assert rhetorical agency, they do so as "an embodied and spatially located form of 'we' among 'us.'"[60] Chávez's study, in particular, tracks the concrete rhetorical practices of multiple protest groups to build coalitions. Accounting for both the oppressive conditions of possibility for these coalitional practices as well as their possibilities to forge alternatives to national citizenship, Chávez helped direct rhetoricians away from studying national citizenship as *the* primary mode of belonging and toward examining belonging as conscious efforts to align with groups who are differentially excluded and recognize the necessity of engaging lawmaking apparatuses to effect positive change.

Extending Rowe's and Chávez's emphases on belonging as a politics of relation rather than a politics of location, this project examines how women's rhetorics of belonging have less to do with accessing, protesting, or responding to belonging as national citizenship. No doubt, national citizenship is not going away anytime soon as the primary state apparatus through which life and death are often made possible. But in light of how globalization has wreaked havoc on women and girls in concrete ways, it seems that centering our scholarly energies on discourses of citizenship might indeed contribute to the rhetorical force of citizenship as the sine qua non of belonging—a belonging with high benefits and high costs. I propose instead viewing national citizenship as one of many rhetorics of belonging to help unsettle the tight link between practices and performances of rhetoric and practices and performances of citizenship. My study of belonging as a rhetoric of relation foregrounds how women imagined new relationships that in turn drew new boundaries of belonging altogether. In turn, they rendered national citizenship as *one way* of belonging to a community—a way that, for many, is an untenable and/or a violent form of belonging. Not only do these rhetorics of belonging render national citizenship as one of many ways to belong, but they also transform what it means to belong to a nation-state in more useful ways to women and girls. The following unpacks how belonging can help wrest the practice of rhetoric away from the practice of national citizenship, especially when discussed in terms of relationships, place, ownership, and constituency.

Often when we talk about belonging, we do so in terms of places. We might say, "I belong to Spain," "they belong over there," or "we belong at home." I contend, however, that these expressions reflect and shape belongings to people and relationships. Explicit statements of belonging to people might sound like, "I belong to you," "we belong to each other," and "you belong with your family." Indeed, we think of our belonging to families as emplaced in the homes, cities, or states where we live with and visit them. Likewise, we think of belonging to the people of regional, national, and global communities as emplaced in the regions, nations, and world where we imagine these people to live and relationships to thrive. Here I emphasize places as socially and rhetorically constituted by the relationships between and among its inhabitants. This view corroborates Thomas Rickert's study of ambient rhetoric that views agency as emplaced, or "activity both occasioned and conditioned by surrounding lands, communities, and forces."[61] Thinking of belonging as emplaced relationships à la Rickert allows critics to view rhetorics of belonging as the "caretaking, shepherding, sparing, or cultivation" of relationships to others that gives meaning and force to places.[62]

Thinking about belonging this way allows us to see how it relates to but does not privilege national citizenship. Declaring, for example, that one belongs to Spain can mean that one is suitable or *proper to* Spain, that one's relationships are emplaced in Spain as an imagined and geographically defined community. It can also mean that one is *property of* Spain, insofar as one's belonging is defined in terms of state-sanctioned rights, privileges, and duties. Critics of nationalism and citizenship may find this assertion consonant with the power of the nation-state to label persons as citizens and noncitizens and, in turn, control bodies through policies of immigration, penal code, deportation, and reproductive rights. A more generous reading speaks to the mutual belonging-to relationship that resonates with liberal theories of citizenship in which the citizen is a rights-bearing, rational-thinking individual who performs "good" citizenship in order to receive certain benefits.

Whether one's assertion of belonging is as proper to or property of a place, it is still primarily an assertion about a relationship. Thinking about belonging in terms of ownership highlights how we can decenter national citizenship from belonging. If we think of "belonging" as a thing one owns, as in, "this home is my belonging," we can imagine that expressions of belonging to a place assert one's ownership of the relationships emplaced in that home. In that sense, one might think of relationships to communities as belongings—as things we take ownership of and ownership in. This reading brings into focus the rhetorical agency of actors and their capacity to speak and be heard as part of the process of creating relationships and places of belonging.

If belonging is limited to national citizenship, then belonging is tightly bound to the nation-state as owner of its citizens. Theoretically, a democracy does not adopt this strict sense of ownership, but as history shows, democracies repeatedly engage in the violent expulsion of undesired populations. It is for this very reason that I urge a reading of national citizenship as one type of belonging. If people reimagine belonging as relationships to one another as members of regional, national, and/or global communities, then they can sidestep and even reconfigure the power of the nation-state to define belonging. Moreover, when relationships are imagined as constitutive of regions and the world, the governing apparatuses of those places can wield more power than that of the state. This is not to suggest that as constituents of regions and the world people can possess unfettered agency, but they can decenter the power of a state apparatus to define who they are and what they can do.

Finally, I want to highlight how decentering belonging as national citizenship can allow people to imagine themselves as ideal constituents of a place. The women under study not only reimagine how they belong, but they also imagine themselves and the women they lead as the necessary change agents of their communities. In all three case studies, this enabled women to move away from factions, nations, and organizations that positioned them as property, mothers, and victims. These reimaginings allowed women to see themselves in relationship with one another as ideal rhetorical actors whose rhetorical practices constituted what it meant to belong. Of course, this rhetorical strategy is also constraining, insofar as positioning one group as an ideal constituency positions other groups as less than ideal. I find, however, that the rhetorics of belonging under study position women as ideal leaders who forged more inclusive communities than their nationalist, male counterparts. In these studies, then, rhetorics of belonging do not function as stringently exclusive rhetorics of citizenship. The following explains how I study rhetorics of belonging in three interrelated case studies of women leaders around the world.

Outline for Study

The women leaders featured in this study reimagine belonging as relationships among women constitutive of a geographically imagined place. In light of the enabling and constraining discourses that shaped their material and symbolic realities, women leaders asserted rhetorical agency through rhetorical practices that constituted anew relationships between women, which in turn repositioned them as members of national, regional, and supranational communities. These reimagined relationships took the forms

of denizenship, cosmopolitanism, and connectivity. As denizens, cosmopolitans, and connectors, women leaders asserted rhetorical agency through
situated rhetorical practices. In turn, the women of their communities, rela-
tional and geographic, were enabled to engage communities in alternative
ways to national citizenship.

Key to understanding these rhetorical transformations is the recognition
that these women leaders did not merely work from within the discourses
of citizenship to include women in national, regional, and global communities. They redefined categories of belonging altogether in ways that presumed,
resisted, and superseded national citizenship such that women could not
only engage their regional, national, and supranational communities in ways
that counted but also rewrite what it meant to belong to a nation in the first
place. This pushback against the singularity and isomorphism of national
citizenship spotlights how women asserted rhetorical agency from within the
constraints and potential of transnational forces at work on geographic and
definitional boundaries of belonging. In all three cases, women leaders redefined belonging in ways that positioned women as the ideal rhetorical actors of
their communities. As regional denizens, national cosmopolitans, and global
connectors, women not only belonged but set a new standard of belonging.

This book's case studies are organized somewhat chronologically, although
some of the time periods of each overlap. More importantly, I organized
these studies to demonstrate how different rhetorics of belonging emerge
depending on the situated exigencies of the woman leaders under study.
Likewise, each case study was selected as emblematic of a particular type
of geographically imagined place: a region, a nation, a world. While each
of the studies articulate a type of belonging to all three places, each articulation foregrounds one in front of the others. In that respect, each of the
case studies can be read independently of the others, but in the proposed
order—regional, national, and then global—the types of imagined relationships build upon one another in terms of women's rights advancements and
in terms of rhetorical practices.

Chapter 1 examines the rhetorical practices of women leaders in West
Africa who forged peace amidst civil warfare. Building upon the idea that
a denizen is someone who frequently visits, inhabits, and/or is adapted to
a certain place, I argue that these women asserted their belonging as denizens of homes, landscapes, peace conferences, and politics. Through their
"dwelling practices," these women enacted belonging to places otherwise
uninhabitable and under threat. In turn, these women transformed their status as violently excluded citizens into agents whose demands and dwelling

practices are the stuff of community belonging. Scholars of political science, social psychology, law, and anthropology typically refer to denizens as resident noncitizens.[63] Most studies of this sort, then, view denizenship as a legal and political status, one that is an incomplete version of citizenship.[64] As denizens of the West Africa region, then, women leaders dislodged themselves from the boundaries of the factions and nations that claimed them as property, and they reformulated the standards by which women belonged. Their rhetorical practices, as embodied assertions of rhetorical agency, included dwelling with each other, with resistant women, and with warlords in homes; traversing the war-torn landscape of Liberia to reestablish flows of food and information and to transform the land from an assemblage of turfs into a nation of networked activists and warlords; inserting themselves into regional peace conferences led and organized by men; mobilizing and uniting women of Christian and Muslim peace networks; and protesting, hovering around, and surrounding spaces of peace talks among male faction leaders. Each of these practices, I argue, represents different forms of dwelling, an act that is temporarily permanent and thus well suited to asserting agency in the in-between moments of transnational movement. The texts under study are autobiographical accounts and published transcripts of interviews with many peace leaders who spoke about their involvement in both Liberian civil wars, spanning from 1990 to 2003.[65] In sum, the women leaders of West Africa's peace networks constituted women's relationships to one another as regional denizens, as inhabitants of dwelling places their practices constituted, where they shaped what it meant to belong to peaceful nations, regions, and the world.[66]

Chapter 2 traces one of the outcomes of this regional movement: the election of Africa's first woman president. Many of the women who led West Africa to peace rallied and mobilized to elect Ellen Johnson Sirleaf as president of Liberia in 2005. As a women's rights advocate and a lifelong Liberian politician, Sirleaf was poised to lead the country out of turmoil and near-total destruction. After fourteen years of civil warfare, Sirleaf needed to craft a brand of national belonging that not only included women as part of the new democracy but also situated them as regional and global leaders, especially in light of the leadership demonstrated throughout Liberia's peace talks. To those ends, Sirleaf constituted women as national cosmopolitans through three rhetorical practices: promoting and normalizing women's rights to supranational and regional governing bodies; advocating for national policy change and initiatives that enabled women as educators free from sexual assault, as policymakers, and as entrepreneurs; and arguing that, through these practices, Liberian women enacted a national cosmopolitan ideal. This analysis draws on Sirleaf's autobiography and her public addresses, from her first inaugural in January 2006 to her last address in 2013.[67] In sum, Sirleaf enabled women's national leadership as necessary to regional and global leadership.

Chapter 3 examines one of the outcomes of African women's demands for peace. Throughout the 1990s and 2000s, African women inserted themselves into different agencies of the United Nations (UN), which culminated in a security resolution that mandated women be included and protected in all peace talks. The successful passage of this resolution did little to stem the politics of supranational organizations and their conferences, which privileged Western, First World ideals of feminist change. The politics of First World or Third World national belonging, then, structured the politics of global governance. Amidst calls for the greater inclusion and representation of non-First World women and a more transnationally adept model of global governance, the UN formed UN Women in 2010. This chapter analyzes Michelle Bachelet's rhetoric as the first Executive Director of UN Women for how it refashioned top-down, globalist relationships between political elites (state representatives, leaders of intergovernmental organizations [IGOs] and nongovernmental organizations [NGOs]) with the women they claim to represent.[68] After serving a term as Chile's first woman president, Bachelet was tasked with directing the new UN agency to support state member governments by mainstreaming gender policy and increasing women's leadership in the UN. In light of these tasks, Bachelet needed to reimagine global belonging away from hierarchical models of global governance toward a model that enabled what Inderpal Grewal termed "transnational connectivity." I argue that Bachelet enacted and promoted rhetorical practices that helped form transnational connectivities between and among political elites and civil-society actors, across national and worldist belongings. Specifically, Bachelet transformed UN Women's annual meetings of the Commission on the Status of Women (CSW) into places where attendees' rhetorical practices forged transnational connectivities generative of transnational change. Her particular rhetorical strategies aimed to reposition attendees as an audience to the women they claim to represent and to validate women's first-person testimonies of abuse and trauma as knowledge and grounds for policy change. In turn, Bachelet modeled for attendees rhetorical practices that validated this knowledge. She narrated her experiences of listening as eager recognition of another's pain and of witnessing oppression as grounds for political action. She also positioned attendees as interlocutors with the women they represent and created the infrastructure to enable attendees to engage in ongoing dialogue and consultation. Last, she constituted attendees as members of a discursive community whose values of inclusion and participation are rehearsed through epideictic occasions that shamed failure and rewarded success. To make this case, I analyze all of Bachelet's speeches from these conferences and at other UN Women meetings. In sum, Bachelet enabled women as rhetorical connectors whose belonging to this global community transcended and shaped their belongings to national and regional communities.

Last, a conclusion argues that because women's belonging in a transnational world is often violently disabused, critics must continue to study how women leaders and their rhetorical imaginings work to enable new modes of belonging. This study's focus on regional, national, and global belonging puts forth concrete rhetorical practices enacted and promoted by women leaders which in turn can be examined, emulated, and circulated toward the greater empowerment of women around the world. Acknowledging the nodal qualities of each case study, as loosely bracketed rhetorical moments and strategies, this book points to how women from different locations—materially, symbolically, and politically—articulated belonging in ways that presuppose and/or subvert the power of national citizenship.

Likewise, these three case studies demonstrate how the enabling and constraining discourses of national citizenship and transnationalism forged interconnected assertions of rhetorical agency. As denizens, for example, women asserted their ability to dwell and inhabit spaces as leaders of a region. As these leaders participated in the election of a woman president, they heightened the exigency for a nationalism that was necessarily inclusive of regional belonging. As cosmopolitans, women's social, economic, and political activities shaped national, regional, and global communities. As such, these women leaders could take up their national and regional concerns in supranational spaces where they could dialogue and shape policy recommendations alongside (and as) political elites. Mapping the ways that these rhetorical practices networked across regional, national, and global communities illustrates how critics can account for the public addresses of women in a transnationalized world without ascribing unmitigated agency to speaker and speech. In other words, these women leaders asserted rhetorical agency from within rhetorical situations that were both unique and part of a shared transnational context.

I

BELONGING AS DENIZENSHIP:
PEACE WOMEN AND REGIONAL DWELLING

In 1994 the Liberian Women's Initiative (LWI) drafted a position paper that documented how the First Liberian Civil War affected women and children. The paper began, "We, the women of Liberia, are the mothers of the land. We feel the joys and sorrows of this land in a special way because we are women. Not only do we represent one half of the population, but we also feel a special sense of responsibility for our children, our husbands and our brothers who make up the other half of the population. We take care of the society. We soothe the pains. We are the healers and the peacemakers."[1] The organization drew on women's social and cultural power as mothers to advance its case for peace. Within the context of war, this is a common rhetorical strategy.[2] Since the rise of the nation-state as the dominant unit of belonging, the nation-as-family metaphor has helped structure social and cultural relations among citizens.[3] Because women are thought to biologically reproduce a nation's citizens, they are therefore positioned as mothers of all the nation's citizens. Moreover, the rise of modern capitalism shaped the home as the primary unit of familial belonging, a place that structured gendered relations such that women were charged with raising their children as ideal citizens, and men were charged with protecting them.[4] Not only does the nation-as-family metaphor stabilize relationships between citizens and the nation-state, but it often justifies military action as protection or defense of home, women, and children or as a violation of an enemy's home turf.

Positioned as mothers of the nation, LWI leaders invoked African women's militant, mystical, and ubiquitous authority. At times of heightened conflict women have often leveraged motherhood as a source of militant action. Their sacred position as mothers—mothers of victims, of the nation, and of the nation's children—justify militant responses to authorities. Various groups of "militant mothers," as scholars have called them, have protested wars and demanded peace in nations all over the world, including Algeria,

Argentina, Chile, El Salvador, Iraq, Japan, South Africa, Spain, the West Bank, and Gaza.[5] As militant mothers, women enacted various forms of embodied confrontation without fear of consequences such as imprisonment, torture, and death.

For LWI members in particular, this militant strength stems from the widely shared belief that African mothers possess mystical powers as "healers" and "peacemakers." Oyeronke Oyewumi argues that African mothers are attributed spiritual and mystical powers for their abilities to endure the physical pain of female circumcision and childbirth.[6] Moreover, these powers are thought to accumulate and intensify over time, constructing older women as particularly influential members of their immediate and broader families.[7] The LWI's appeal to the maternal and mystical powers of African women was inextricably linked to cultural understandings of "family" as a wider kinship network that can span villages, towns, and regions. "Family" isn't limited to parents and their biological offspring, nor is it limited to a single place, like a home or a nation. Family can include immediate and distant relatives; adopted children or parents; and members across the same indigenous group, religion, and/or village.[8] In fact, in many African societies, older women must be addressed as "Auntie" or "Ma" in deference to their authority as mothers who help raise, educate, and heal the children of their families and kin across village, town, and national borders.[9]

The LWI position paper's first sentence, "We, the women of Liberia, are the mothers of the land," is prismatic of these maternal appeals. As "mothers of the land," they situate themselves as mothers of the nation, as mothers who must militantly protect the land, and as mothers whose mystical powers make them especially capable of protecting the extended families who inhabit the land. Altogether, however, these maternal appeals don't fully account for the rhetorical force of this claim. To be sure, "the land" can refer the physical places and landscapes where mothers work and dwell within the boundaries of homes, churches, urban centers, villages, and nation. In another sense, "land" is nonlocal. They say, "We feel the joys and sorrows of this land in a special way because we are women," inflecting these places and landscapes with "joys and sorrows"—amorphous, ubiquitous, nonconcrete things. Thus these women are mothers who belong to "the land," a bounded and yet boundary-less place where they "feel," "take care," "soothe," heal, and make peace.

As they engaged in those practices throughout "the land," the women of the LWI and other peace activists enacted a different kind of belonging: denizenship. When civil warfare displaced Liberians from homes and villages and when citizenship as belonging became violently defended and enforced, women enacted denizenship and in the process asserted belonging as denizens, people who frequently inhabit, visit, and dwell in places, both geographic and imagined. That is, denizens engage in rhetorical dwelling practices to belong to places. These "peace women," as I call them, organized, traveled, mediated, lobbied, pleaded, interrupted, protested, sang, danced, and prayed for peace. These rhetorical acts constitute dwelling places, the places where or in which peace women asserted belonging. Sometimes dwelling practices constituted dwelling places that were actual homes—homes of sympathizers and warlords. But more often dwelling places were public and political places: dirt roads, streets, parking lots, fields, lobbies, hallways, and rooms at peace conferences. They were also nonliteral places, such as "in" and "through" the relationships forged through the shared experience of enacting denizenship. As denizens of Liberia, the peace women belonged to the land in ways that citizenship otherwise denied them.

This chapter primarily focuses on how Liberian women enacted denizenship. Throughout the 1990s and early 2000s, Liberian women organized into a myriad of peace organizations, coalitions, and loosely affiliated activists to stem civil warfare in the West Africa region.[10] They worked amidst the political, ethnic, and military conflicts of West Africa's Mano River Union countries, which include Guinea, Côte d'Ivoire, and Sierra Leone. Liberia suffered two civil wars across fourteen years (1989–97, 1999–2003), although a coup in 1980 set off a decade of unrest before civil warfare officially began.[11] Within the first year of Liberia's first civil war, seven hundred thousand Liberians fled to Sierra Leone. Sierra Leone's civil war dates from March 23, 1991, when the Revolutionary United Front (RUF) began its overthrow of the government, to January 18, 2002, when the government declared the war over.[12] By September 1997, two hundred thousand Sierra Leoneans had fled to Liberia for refuge. During Liberia's second civil war, then dictator Charles Taylor manipulated political and military conflicts to gain influence in the surrounding Mano River Union countries and to undermine and attack Economic Community of West African States (ECOWAS) forces who had trained in Freetown, Sierra Leone.[13] During these conflicts, shared borders between Guinea, Sierra Leone, and Liberia became sites of struggle between multiple military and political factions who launched attacks on villages of all three countries.[14] To manage border insecurity, Taylor strategically supported rebel troops in Guinea and Sierra Leone.[15] He supplied RUF with armed forces, hoping to capitalize on arms trade and on Sierra Leone's diamond districts located along shared borders.[16] Within one month RUF and Taylor's special forces had secured control of wide swaths of eastern Sierra Leone.[17] In turn, Sierra Leonean combatants fought with Taylor's National Patriotic Front of Liberia throughout the 1990s.

These civil wars and intraregional conflicts are considered the result of the unchecked power of male dictators, male politicians, male soldiers and rebels, and at least fifteen thousand Liberian and ten thousand Sierra Leonean child soldiers forced to rape, mutilate, and kill their own family members.[18] Notably, girls comprised at least 30 percent of child soldiers, and women made up 30–50 percent of soldiers and rebels.[19] Whether fighting or not, hundreds of thousands of women and girls suffered sexual and psychological abuses throughout the civil wars.[20] Groups of soldiers and rebels posed a daily threat to the lives and livelihoods of Liberians, who were terrorized through murder, displacement, and imprisonment.

Within these symbolically and violently enforced boundaries and constraints, peace women employed rhetorical dwelling practices to persuade other women, rebels, soldiers, and political elites to view them as legitimate actors and, in turn, to view their demands as reasonable. Careful not to identify *every* act as a dwelling practice and *every* place as a dwelling, this chapter views a dwelling practice as any rhetorical act that enables belonging to a place, relationship, or political process without regard for the political and violent enforcement of state-recognized belonging. Dwelling practices transform sites into dwelling places without regard for the political or violent power structures that govern boundaries of belonging. First, peace women dwelled with each other and with men inside homes. In these places, dwelling practices included hosting women who traveled to and from peace meetings, planning and dialoguing with them, sitting with and comforting reluctant and fearful women, and, when summoned by faction leaders, showing up and listening to them. In turn, peace women transformed homes, however violated, as potential places for mediation and dwelling together. Second, peace women enacted dwelling within national boundaries. As they walked, drove, networked, carried and delivered letters between male faction leaders, they transformed the nation's material and symbolic landscape from a set of turfs to a site of networks and relationships. Third, peace women dwelled on the perimeters of political spaces as they gathered, lobbied, and sat in hallways and conference rooms to assert belonging to peacemaking processes. As they observed, listened, mediated, and regulated, they transformed the places of peacemaking politics into places where multiple actors—oppressors, victims, peace activists—dwelled and healed together. At times, peace women enacted militant dwelling in public spaces. They blocked, marched, threatened, chanted, sang, danced, and prayed, to assert their belonging to a peaceful nation where their demands were the stuff of nation building. Often peace women of different organizations employed these three types of rhetorical dwelling practices concurrently, depending on the urgency and simultaneity of different crises in different places. The more elite group of activists of the Mano River Women of Peace Network (MARWOPNET), for example, practiced dwelling within spaces of politics, while the group of more indigenous women, Women in Peace Network (WIPNET), focused on militant dwelling practices, disrupting political processes through mass protests. Toward the end of the conflict, however, these three types of rhetorical dwelling exhibited an accumulative effect in which the escalation to militant dwelling depended on the simultaneous practice of dwelling in homes, across landscapes, and in politics. Through these strategies, peace women dwelled with men, earned their trust, and successfully brought men together and forged peace. Additionally, peace women innovated dwelling practices to persuade women of all classes and religions to engage in peace activism and, in turn, emboldened them to assert belonging to a peaceful nation as well as to the political processes through which peace is built.

To make this case, this chapter examines the first- and secondhand testimonies of women who participated in the peacemaking processes throughout the Liberian civil wars. While a number of countries and women's groups were active during the extensive history of conflicts between and among Mano River Union countries, ethnic groups, and political factions, a focus on how Liberian women negotiated these boundaries allows for an examination of how peace women asserted belonging to their country, as well as to the region, particularly as they dwelled with women across ethnic, religious, and national lines. Because many of these peace women did not have the means to record their activities in real time, I analyze their narratives through autobiographical accounts and through interviews conducted one or two years after the civil wars ended. A handful of scholars, journalists, nonprofit organizations, and UN agencies collected these interviews. The most comprehensive study, and the one I draw on most heavily, compiled interviews of "Liberian women peace activists" who were "identified by women and men, both in Liberia and outside it, who had been closely involved in peace processes" (*LWP*, vi). The book *Liberian Women Peacemakers* provides ninety-four pages of women's firsthand accounts, situated in their political and social contexts, pieced together through interviews, and supplemented by news and scholarly sources. Scarcity of resources and fear of retribution limited the kinds of texts available to study how peace women imagined and forged belonging to places and nations. Moreover, the compilers of the interviews acknowledge that the people interviewed "are not intended to be a perfect research sample" as they tend to favor the experiences of women in Monrovia, rather than rural women who suffered in isolation "due to the inaccessibility of large parts of the country during the war" (xi). Representing, to an extent, the experiences of rural women, Leymah Gbowee's autobiography, *Mighty Be Our Powers: How Sisterhood, Prayer, and Sex Changed a Nation at War*, offers her memory of peace activism during the second civil war. Fully aware that these texts put forward partial and backward-looking narratives, I consider these as primary texts insofar as they bear the imprint of how peace women have come to make sense of their actions and how they shaped their precarious contexts.

When coupled with news reports and scholarly sources, these texts create an assemblage of views on how women suffered and survived civil warfare. In no way do I attempt to offer an "official" or "complete" story of how women brokered peace. This analysis is necessarily skewed by the variety of goals and work women's organizations undertook, including providing food, shelter, and counseling to victims; physically confronting warlords; and demanding peace. This variation constrains my analysis from drawing conclusions about particular rhetorical strategies suited to particular goals. On the other hand, with this imperfect collection of artifacts, I am able to draw conclusions about the common dwelling practices *across* different groups who, through caretaking, mediation, and/or confrontation, sought to bring peace to individuals, communities, and nations.

As a rhetorical critic, I acknowledge the partiality and incompleteness of all texts and my impulse to assemble certain texts and not others, to arrange them so their rough edges and corners brush up against each other, overlap, and gap, and to read them through my own feminist sensibilities, asking over and over: How did these women suffer? How did they dwell? How did they insist on their belonging? The following analysis answers these questions by first elucidating the relationships between belonging, dwelling, and rhetorical dwelling practices. Then an analysis illustrates how peace women perceived themselves as denizens engaged in multiple dwelling practices, particularly as they dwelled in homes, dwelled in the nation, and dwelled in politics. Last, the conclusion draws out the potential and pitfalls of denizenship as a way to belong in a transnational world.

Belonging and Dwelling

In a strictly legal sense, citizenship is supposed to guarantee belonging to a nation one might consider home. However, in our current transnational milieu, amidst increasingly rapid flows of migrants, workers, and refugees, classical notions of citizenship fail to explain both what *citizenship* means and how to live in a nation after (forcibly or not) leaving one's nation of origin or place they might call home.[21] Many scholars have embraced "denizenship" as a political, legal, and/or a social status that better captures how vulnerable populations craft belonging to communities outside the borders of their nation of origin and within the borders of another. *Denizens* refers to those who lie somewhere between fully enfranchised citizens and long-term residents. The concepts of "denizen" and "denizenship" trace back to the thirteenth century, when "deni" denoted inner part, inner, and within.[22] It follows that, as a political and legal designation, a "denizen" is a "resident noncitizen" or an unnaturalized person whom the state recognizes and allows to live and dwell within their national boundaries.[23] Although denizens are denied certain rights, such as the right to vote, they can access various civil, social, and economic rights, such as access to public education, health care, and welfare.[24]

Despite—and because of—this precarious political status, denizens' belonging is always already defined within *and* against a national community. Often denizens forge and define a community of belonging for themselves. Political scientists have theorized different ways in which denizens have asserted their agency within the precarious conditions of their belonging. In their view, resident noncitizens can enact "negotiated denizenship" and "substantive denizenship" to access basic rights from the state and in turn forge a fortified community of belonging within certain neighborhoods and urban enclaves.[25] For example, one study examined a group of denizens in England who capitalized on living in an enclave of state-sponsored housing, however impoverished, and by refusing to sign on for unemployment benefits. This way denizens formed a cash-in-hand underground economy, kept "money on the manor," and escaped state oversight.[26] While some denizens had become naturalized British citizens, all strategically identified as outsiders living within the state.[27] Thus, denizenship is not only a political, legal, and social status, it is also a rhetorically constructed and maintained identity—one that shapes and is shaped by the conditions that enable denizens to dwell in particular nations and places.

This chapter in particular examines home as a site of dwelling practices that assert and transform what it means to belong as denizens. Much social theory has explored the relationship between dwelling as a place and as human practice. Notably, Heidegger's essay "Building Dwelling Thinking" proposes that we build places in which to dwell and in the practice of dwelling, we are human.[28] He says, "I dwell, you dwell. The way in which we are and I am, the manner in which we are humans on earth, is *Buan*, dwelling."[29] However, this relationship between dwelling, humanity, and home has undergone substantial critique. Many scholars argue that Heidegger helped "dissociate 'dwelling' and 'being-at-homeness'" such that the home is thought to be a "distinct human space" that exists apart from "the spaces of mobility and labor."[30] Critiques of Heidegger's notion of dwelling and home rightly highlight his romanticization of home as a secure, stable, safe place for rumination and development of the self.[31] Considering that this conceptualization of dwelling relies on the labor of marginalized persons—women, children, servants, slaves—groups who often don't count as "human," it can reify masculinist, nationalist, and capitalist ideologies of personhood and belonging.[32]

Theorists interested in dwelling as a practice of citizenship within the current context of transnationalism have begun to view home less as a place of being human and more as a set of practices that define a place as home. Because practicing dwelling isn't necessarily tied to a singular or permanent place, one can practice dwelling to forge belonging to places that may or may not count as "home." As James N. Rosenau put it, transnational theorists view home as "the lived experience of locality—a/the locality enters ourselves through the senses (sound, smell, touch) and the self penetrates locality in equally sensual ways."[33] Likewise, Stuart Hall disabused the concept of dwelling in/as a fixed place as he proposed "dwelling-in-traveling" and "traveling-in-dwelling."[34] The former idea asks how one maintains strong cultural ties and identities while traveling (primarily for "traveling cultures"), while the latter explores how we can engage in cultural traveling while dwelling in place. In short, these theorists posit "home" as within and without the self who shapes and is shaped by concrete experiences in particular locations.

These more contemporary senses of "home" help destabilize the modernist underpinnings of Heidegger's "dwelling" but continue to presume an individual that moves freely to create "homes" where they wish. This presumption, like Heidegger's romanticization of home, ignores the political and material realities that dictate who, where, and how some individuals may dwell. As Davika Chawla and Stacy Holman Jones note, "a large percentage of women, children, and young persons experience home—as a place of terror, a site of fear and isolation, and often as a prison."[35] They continued, "In our era of forced and continuous global migrations we are all keenly aware that home and homemaking can also be a destabilizing, disabling, and disembodying experience."[36]

To problematize the association of home with "stasis, boundaries, identity[,] and fixity" and with being "a purified space of belonging," Sara Ahmed compares the home to the nation where "there are always encounters with others already recognized as strangers within, rather than just between, nation spaces."[37] In her view, "there is always an encounter with strangerness, even within the home: the home does not secure identity by expelling strangers, but requires those strangers to establish relations of proximity and distance within the home. . . . There is always strangeness and movement within the home itself."[38] One's dwelling practices, then, will always be enabled and constrained by a home's shifting political, social, and economic power dynamics. Seen this way, belonging to a home—as a structure, a village, a nation—is an ongoing process of encountering the familiar as strange and the strange as familiar.

These "dwelling practices," as Emily McKee calls them, are the means through which people "of contested landscapes vie over land and resources."[39] This concept accounts for the tight relationship between the physical contours of place and nation—homes, halls, roads, rivers—and their rhetorical significance as sites for the practices of dwelling. To augment McKee's account of how dwelling practices enable people to "stake claims" to land and "negotiate large-scale power struggles" in local and concrete ways, I view these practices as inherently rhetorical insofar as they are symbolic and embodied practices at work to forge belonging to the places and the nations in which they occur.[40] According to Nedra Reynolds, dwelling is both a noun and a verb; dwellings are not only "the places we most intimately or frequently occupy," but dwelling is also "a set of practices as well as a sense of place."[41] These practices are inclusive of the movement, shuttling, and crossing of borders that constitute and transform specific locales and nations into dwelling places wherein people relate, inhabit, and dwell together.

Viewing home as a site of dwelling practices helps us see how those without a place or a nation to call home, traditionally defined, can forge belonging. Moreover, it allows us to view the in-between—the shuttling, the crossing, and the migrating—not as the means to belong to a place or a nation but as enactments of belonging that transform places into *dwelling* places, places where belonging is enabled through practice, not state-recognized status. As Kathy-Ann Tan contests, this focus rejects "the dominant point of view that denizens occupy a space of marginality in the nation-state, which relies on a center-periphery model."[42] Rather, this focus embraces the view that denizens already inhabit, dwell within, and can belong.

West African Peace Women and Dwelling

Analyzing the dwelling practices of West African peace women spotlights how these women asserted belonging to each other, to the political processes of peacemaking, and to a peaceful nation. They opened up their homes to each other and offered temporary dwelling places for rest and organizations, transforming violated and/or susceptible homes into sites where members of an extended family can belong. They dwelled with faction leaders in homes, transforming threatening places into places where trust is earned. They traversed the war-torn terrain of Liberia to negotiate with faction leaders; to carve roads; and to enable flows of food, goods, and information, transforming the landscape from a set of turfs into a network of negotiated relationships. They insinuated themselves into places of peacemaking, transforming peace conferences from sites of power wrangling into sites of grieving and relationship building. Likewise, they dwelled militantly in public and on the periphery of peace negotiations, occupying places reserved for political and public goings-on, transforming sites of deliberation into places where women must assert their voices.

Dwelling in Homes

Within and across economic, social, and political categories, West African women have always negotiated power as "providers, feeders, and sustainers of the household" and by extension, of the village, the town, the nation, and the region.[43] That said, homes are not necessarily sites of unmitigated agency. West African women are often situated within structures of male domination that make the "home" a locus of male sexual control. Thus, their dwelling practices may assert belonging to their homes, while simultaneously their homes can be sites of power struggles and sexual violence.

Civil warfare magnifies this paradox. In Liberia soldiers and rebels infiltrated the homes of civilians and peace leaders, seeking to rape, murder, or to intimidate peace women into giving information. While "home" doesn't necessarily represent places of safety and comfort for dwellers, once infiltrated and violated, whatever sense of security and comfort it offered is likewise infiltrated and violated. Some violations were indiscriminate. Toward the end of the conflict, for example, when official peacekeeping forces arrived in Monrovia, rebels engaged in what was called a "frenzy of rape" in which they went door to door attacking girls and women ages eight to sixty-five (*LWP*, 51). A firsthand account described rebels as "wild-eyed men" who burst into one home, raped a ten-year-old girl, and left "her lying in a pool of blood and vomit—dead." In the same home, gunmen raped a fourteen-year-old girl and bludgeoned the girl's mother (51).

In other instances, soldiers and rebels targeted the homes and offices of peace workers, forcing many to abandon these places and leave the country altogether (32). Clara d'Almeida, for example, reflected on a time when, following a day of mediation with rebel leaders, a number of "armed combatants" showed up on her doorstep at midnight: "I don't know how they found my house, but one of the men knocked on my door. He was a frontline commander. I said, 'Who is that?' and he said, 'I'm so and so.' I said, 'So and so? How did you find my house?' He said 'There is nowhere in Monrovia we can't find if we want to'" (13). Fortunately, the encounter was peaceful; the men sat and talked with her on her porch. Nonetheless, the encounter disrupted the notion that Clara's home was a safe place of retreat and, moreover, proved that no place was sacred or impervious to threat.

As discussed earlier, a home is a place consecrated by dwelling practices, both comforting and discomforting, strange and familiar.[44] Disruptions to one's dwelling practices make the comfortable strange, while they simultaneously create the conditions of possibility to make the strange comfortable. Through a set of dwelling practices centered on peacemaking, Liberian women worked to make the strange comfortable as they created new homes in which activists could belong. Sierra Leonean women who lived along the Liberian border, for example, "drew upon their experience running large households" and opened up their homes to Liberian refugees who needed shelter—sometimes thirty refugees to a home (7, 15). These women also opened their homes to peacemakers en route to Freetown for peace talks, so they could rest or hold strategic planning sessions (15). In these instances, women practiced dwelling as hosting and dialoguing, even if for a night, to craft a vision for the future and to assert that they belonged to each other and to a home.

Women not only dwelled together in the homes of sympathizers, but they also practiced dwelling in the homes of women who resisted peacemaking activities. Rural women were particularly hesitant to speak about the atrocities of war; often they feared retribution from their perpetrators. Poor and uneducated, they had little recourse for the abuses they endured. Thus, peace leaders needed to assuage their fears of speaking about their abuses and their needs. Leaders encouraged some of these women to represent other rural women and speak to faction leaders about their needs. Ruth Caesar, for example, reflected, "We put our arms around them. I would go to communities, sit down with the women in their houses and find out their problems.

The strategy was to show care for people, telling them they too are part of the process. . . . We made them feel relaxed and comfortable so much that they were able to articulate what they wanted" (64). Caesar engaged in the dwelling practices of sitting and listening so that women could "feel relaxed and comfortable" in their own homes—homes that had been violated by the abuses they had endured. In Sara Ahmed's words, these women formed a community "by sharing the lack of a home rather than sharing a home."[45] Caesar redefined these women's homes as shared dwelling places for women seeking peace.

Likewise, peace leaders engaged in dwelling practices with faction leaders. In early 1994 women formed a delegation of leaders that represented rural and urban women who then lobbied faction leaders for meetings and moderated those meetings so that faction leaders agreed to dialogue with each other (12–17). During this time of conflict, individual meetings with faction leaders were always on the men's terms, precipitated by their political whims, and therefore took place on demand. Because of this unpredictability, Caesar recalled, "Theresa Leigh-Sherman would have her bag packed, and when her phone rang and they said, 'Come, Mr. Warring Faction A can see you immediately,' she picked up her bag. She was ever ready" (65). She was always prepared to meet with others in a new place—even places where she was vulnerable to violence. Caesar and others also met with these men. They practiced dwelling as they listened, talked, and proposed meetings for mediation. In turn, their practices constituted dwelling places where men felt they could gather. In Caesar's words, one man thought, "Well, if we are going to meet together, we will meet under the leadership of women" (64). Indeed, their notions of how dwelling can be practiced and where dwelling can happen successfully crafted belonging to homes, to each other, *and* with faction leaders in productive ways.

Dwelling in the Landscape of the Nation

Many women argue that the trust and goodwill they earned with faction leaders enabled them to travel between villages and the turfs of different factions. Through their dwelling practices, as activist Evelyn Kandakai puts it, "women could maneuver a little more than men," and as Senator Evelyn Townsend observes, women "were able to go where many people dared not go" (*LWP*, 28, 73). This was the case not only for dwelling in homes, but also for dwelling within the geographic boundaries of the nation. To peace activists, dwelling together within houses, rooms, and on porches transformed homes into places of belonging. Likewise, dwelling together within the nation's borders, across its roads, along its rivers, and between its villages transformed the nation from a confederation of turfs into a place of movement, relationships, and belonging for the dispossessed.

As the women traveled great distances across Liberia, they engaged in the dwelling practices that asserted belonging to the nation. Specifically, the women dwelled together through walking, shuttling, and driving across and into the turfs of various factions. They sought to "establish lines of communication between rival factions, transitional governments, ECOWAS, ECOMOG [Economic Community of West African States Monitoring Group] and other actors" (22). Activist Mary Brownell recalls, "We visited almost all the African countries wherever there was a peace conference going on. There was a time when we even carried letters and hand delivered them to the different warlords" (22). Martha Nagbe, farmer and businesswoman, describes the threat they posed to factions' turf: "I worked for peace with LWI, NAWOCOL [National Women's Commission of Liberia], Women Action for Good Will, Concern[ed] Women['s Organization]. . . . We went round from village to village to talk with those boys to put the gun down. We went to Po River, to Mount Barclay, to Lofa, even to the border. . . . The hardest was when we went to Po River. They almost kill us" (83). Recalling how they went "village to village" and "*even* to the border,*" where the boy soldiers almost killed them, Nagbe highlights how women were willing to "transcend customary boundaries" and move "beyond safer havens" (9, 83). After visiting Po River, for example, where the boy soldiers threatened rape, the women pressed on and as Nagbe said, decided they couldn't give up (83). As they walked, drove, and carried and delivered letters, the women transgressed turf lines and asserted their belonging to a nation, a place where women can engage in these dwelling practices. Ultimately, Nagbe says, "women were a little more flexible and courageous [than men]" (73).

In turn, women's rhetorical dwelling practices shaped the Liberian landscape—its gravel roads, undeveloped terrain, and remote villages—as their home through "micropractices" of belonging. According to McKee, people engage in these "micropractices" to assert belonging to landscapes and their attendant geopolitics; they "plant trees, build houses, and till fields."[46] Likewise, she identifies what might be termed "macropractices," or "large-scale power struggles and political maneuverings" that ensure "hierarchies [are] encrusted in the roads, fields, and fences around them."[47] For example, the "frenzy of rape" and destruction that took place in 2003 was the result of a macropractice in which, far away in Accra, Ghana, Charles Taylor went back on his promise to step down from the presidency. Instead, he vowed, "We will never desert the city! We will fight street to street, house to house!"[48] Leymah Gbowee described Monrovia's urban landscape, its roads and streets, in the wake of the attacks: "Days of bombardment left more blocks burned, pavement strewn with rubble, trash, piles of broken furniture. . . . People ran on carpets of shell casings" (*MBOP*, 157). In this case, Taylor's macropractices of war negotiations littered Monrovia's main roads so much that the broken concrete and debris blocked all roads out of the city.

Women activists challenged these encrusted hierarchies through micropractices, particularly as they negotiated and reestablished the flows of food, goods, and information between isolated communities, often closed off by rebels and soldiers. In 1992, for example, United Liberation Movement for Democracy (UNLIMO) forces captured and blocked off Kakata, shutting down a main artery between Gbarnga and Monrovia. Local chapters of the Concerned Women's Organization worked with local market women along the route to gather "large quantities of foodstuffs" and negotiate with warring faction, National Patriotic Front of Liberia, to cross checkpoints into Kakata. Once they arrived, United Liberation Movement for Democracy soldiers met them with raised guns. After several hours of negotiation, the women were allowed access to the road. They went on to negotiate fifty different checkpoints with forces while they also "had to cope with roads that had been devastated by the conflict, [which] slow[ed] progress of the journey considerably" (*LWP*, 10–11). The journey, however slow and physically challenging, reshaped the landscape of Liberia to reestablish a flow of life-saving goods to displaced and isolated people. Through their dwelling practices—traveling, crossing, meeting, negotiating—the women dwelled together within Liberia as a dwelling place, transforming the landscape from one of multiple turfs to one of a nation where the oppressed not only belonged but also functioned as the veins and arteries that connected disparate lands and groups together. The women forged geographic and symbolic connections between rival groups for the good of the Liberian people.

Through these rhetorical dwelling practices, relationships and networks between peace women blossomed. Forging networks across Liberia's terrain—literal and figurative—shaped and was shaped by what activist Etweda Cooper referred to as a "grapevine" of information, carved by "roadrunners" who spread information across multiple communities within hours. According to Ruth Caesar, calls for meetings and strategic planning sessions could amass seventy-five to eighty women within half a day (*LWP*, 14). Indeed, throughout the 1990s, peace leaders attended the 1995 UN World Conference on Women and founded Africa's first NGO dedicated to women's leadership in conflict resolution, Femmes Africa Solidarité, which forged regional and international alliances with the UN Development Fund for Women, the UN High Commissioner for Refugees, and the UN Development Programme (43–44). Eventually, women leaders created a peace organization dedicated specifically to ending civil warfare in West Africa. They built upon the network of the Mano River Union (MRU), a customs union formed in 1974 to enhance economic relationships between the West African nations of Liberia, Sierra Leone, and Guinea (43–45). MRU worked closely with ECOWAS to address social, health, political, and economic issues in the region. Over the course of two ECOWAS-sponsored mediations in Abuja, Nigeria, one in November 1999 and the other in May 2000, fifty-six women formed MARWOPNET. The network's purpose was to establish "a culture of peace" in the MRU nations. Specifically, MARWOPNET leaders "urged ECOWAS to help establish a secure environment through monitoring small arms trafficking, addressing disarmament and developing programs for child soldiers, planning programs for those traumatized by war and encouraging women's self reliance through training in entrepreneurial skills. To ensure their long-term concerns for peace, the women also proposed that the ECOWAS mechanism for conflict resolution be amended to allow three positions for women at high levels" (44–45). The collective power of MARWOPNET leaders helped advance a clear vision of empowering women and children traumatized by civil warfare. Moreover, they advocated for women's political belonging and legitimacy in ECOWAS's decision-making processes.

Three years later, as death and destruction peaked, the women of WIPNET forged belonging to the nation and to the region through similar networking practices. WIPNET's leader, Gbowee, recalls that to assemble women on very short notice, one of WIPNET's core leaders, Grace, trekked wherever necessary to disperse messages and collect protesters: "If you gave her letters to deliver, she would get them where they needed to go, even if she had to walk there. If you needed to assemble a crowd of women, she would find them—she would talk to anyone" (*MBOP*, 139). WIPNET's leaders, who saw themselves as the indigenous counterparts to MARWOPNET's more elite members, traveled great lengths on foot to bring women to Monrovia to participate in what became the historic Liberian Mass Action for Peace campaign. Between April and August 2003, these women leaders' rhetorical dwelling practices responded to the rapidly unfolding crises of the war. According to Gbowee, "None of us had imagined things might happen this quickly, and we had no real plans: everything was being invented day by day" (139). Gbowee describes WIPNET's grassroots and often impromptu efforts: "Grace and a few others went out into different communities passing out flyers. Mariama provided transportation for women in the displaced persons camps who wanted to talk to the press. On April 5, almost one hundred women arrived in Monrovia" (134). In this instance, women leaders forged paths to enable the flow of women and their political power into Monrovia. Asserting their belonging to Liberia, women leaders' dwelling practices included traveling and networking across the war-torn landscape and amassing and shuttling other women in order to demand participation in political processes. Belonging as denizens, peace women reshaped the literal and political landscape of Liberia.

Dwelling Inside and Outside Politics: The First Civil War

As peace leaders organized and forged networks across Liberia's geographic and political terrain, they generated enough trust to enter the political spaces reserved for peace negotiations facilitated and attended by men. That said, between 1990 and 1993, women could attend but not participate in peace conferences.[49] To assert their belonging to peace conferences as active participants, women activists transformed hallways and conference rooms into dwelling places where they asserted their belonging as inhabitants of conferences and of Liberia. They exploited the potential for hallways and conference rooms to function as what Tan calls "insurgent spaces" or "contact zones" that "generate and witness emergent forms of subjectivity and belonging, even as these 'assertion[s] of legitimacy' are challenged and renegotiated."[50] Tan argues that these are insurgent spaces "wherein denizens' demands for recognition are made and claims to belonging are staked."[51] Considering that hallways are places for transition and movement, they can be ideal places to demand attention and legitimacy. Peace women practiced dwelling as they disrupted the movement and flow of others in hallways and lobbies as well as the flow of conference events. These dwelling practices transformed peace conferences into dwelling places.

To illustrate, in December 1994, women raised funds to attend the Accra Clarification Conference held in Ghana, but ECOWAS denied their request for invitations. According to Massa Washington, ECOWAS "thought we were joking, so we proceeded to invite ourselves" (LWP, 24). On the first day of the conference, they sat in a hallway outside the doors of the conference room so they could lobby participants during breaks. At the same time, Washington used her media contacts in Ghana to expose the women's exclusion. Both strategies worked, and the women were granted observer status for the second

day, during which they could only sit, listen, analyze, and "identify possibilities for advocacy and mediation." They continued to stop, interrupt, and peti-
tion participants during breaks, and by the third day, they had been granted
official participant status (24). Asserting their right to belong, these women
waited and lobbied until they entered the inner spaces of peace negotiations.

To ensure participant status at the next peace conference, leaders of LWI
engaged in dwelling practices of writing, traveling, and meeting. Amelia Ward
and Ruth Caesar formed a coalition of women's organizations and everyday
women to draft a formal position paper on the effect of war on women and
children. To this end, hundreds of women collaborated to propose a comprehensive, factual document to present at the next ECOWAS conference (24–
25). While they had hoped the document provided a legitimate case for their
inclusion, they were denied tickets to attend the ECOWAS Heads of State
Mediation Committee meeting in May 1995. Undeterred, Theresa Leigh-
Sherman, Evelyn Townsend, and Clara d'Almeida traveled to the conference.
Arriving without money and barely enough clothes to wear, they set out to
get their paper on the agenda. Before the beginning of the conference, they
met with heads of state, international representatives, and ECOWAS officials
to no avail. Through these dwelling practices, they asserted their belonging
to the conference—whether or not their efforts would result in official recognition of belonging to the peacemaking process.

During his opening remarks, ECOWAS president Jerry Rawlings made
an impromptu change to the agenda and invited the women on stage to present their position paper. Leigh-Sherman recalled, "I just took that paper and
slowly we talked about the killing and how these men were opening these
women's stomachs and betting on the babies. We talked about everything
because the women were tired. It was a 30-minute paper. We made recommendations. And I tell you the nine Presidents that were there and CNN,
BBC, everybody was in tears because these are facts that these people didn't
know about. But we had gone through it. We had lost everything we had
worked for" (26). Provocatively, the paper recommended disarmament and
inclusion of women in all peace talks (27). The women successfully achieved
the latter. D'Almeida recalls the effects of their paper:

> The men and women in that hall cried because they had never heard
> that story told. The only thing they were hearing about is who wants
> to rule, who wants to do this, but what they were doing, the atroci-
> ties going on, they never heard about them. . . . And that's when the
> whole conference made a turn, and it became a different conference.

It focused now on the atrocities that were happening. The next [peace] meeting that was held, we were invited. We were now recognized as people who had something to say—more than washing dishes and taking care of children. (69)

The women transformed the conference hall into a shared dwelling place in which certain dwelling practices—insisting on belonging, addressing reluctant audiences, listening and crying together—shifted the purpose of the conference from who gets what turf to how atrocities must be stopped. In this sense, d'Almeida, Leigh-Sherman, Townsend, and conference participants engaged in what Susan Wittig Albert calls "the difficult work of place-making," or the process of "becoming inhabitants, not quite native, yet, perhaps, somehow kin."[52]

Perceived of as "kin," the women were invited to return to Abuja in July and lead a mediation. Throughout both civil wars, women's dwelling practices often positioned women as mothers to the men, mothers whose jobs were to gather, mediate, and regulate the men's participation.[53] Per ECOWAS's request, the women used their established relationships with faction leaders to bring the men together. As these women visited the homes of faction leaders, made food available to starving communities, and cared for the traumatized, they self-identified as mothers caring for the nation's children and reprimanded men as poorly behaved children. When asked why he attended the mediation, one leader said, "when your mother calls, you listen" (28).

The mediation in July 1995 was no exception. Clara d'Almeida describes how mediation strategies infantilized the men:

Elizabeth Mulbah did some sort of reconciliation thing, starting from scratch, as if they were all children again. It was a beautiful program. . . . She was talking to them, reading to them, playing different games with them. At one time she had pieces of paper which [they] wrote on and turned face down. Everybody was supposed to pick one with somebody's name and say something nice to that person. Can you imagine these people who had been fighting each other all along and all of a sudden have to tell each other something nice? When we first got in there it was as if everybody was ready for a fight. Gradually we saw them simmering down. By the time the conference was over, people were able to stand up and pat each other on the back. . . . And at the end of the meeting they softened the position that they were all holding. . . . To me that was the breaking point of what we have today. (29)

The mediators not only facilitated the men's participation, but they also regulated them, ensuring that participants remained committed to the process of mediation. One mediator recalled how she intercepted a faction leader who became angry and attempted to leave: "'My man where are you going?' I asked. 'That man said something,' he replied. 'Never mind. Just come back because this is Liberia we are talking about. It is greater than all of you'" (28–29). In this instance the mediator not only asserted her maternal authority as a way to dwell within the spaces of peacemaking, but she also asserted her maternal authority as a way to dwell within the nation. In other words, she knew what was good for the men *and* for the nation.

The effects of dwelling together throughout the 1990s, particularly as men and women spent more time in the same dwelling places and engaged in shared dwelling practices, crystallized in Ruth Sando Perry's selection as Head of the Council of State in 1996. Perry, a former senator and peace activist, is often credited for ensuring a peaceful presidential election in 1997. The selection process and her leadership illustrate both the tenuous conditions under which women could dwell with men in political spaces and the agency they could assert to practice dwelling from a position of considerable power.

Perry's ascension to Head of the Council of State is remarkable considering that she was initially excluded from the conference where she was selected. In August 1996 she arrived in Abuja for a peace conference. Although she arrived as a member of a political delegation, she was told she could not be accredited and therefore could not attend. She consulted the Chief of Protocol, who said nothing could be done. After Perry and the Chief witnessed a group of boys receive accreditation, he was embarrassed. According to Perry, "He told the man [at the accreditation table], 'Look, you have to let this woman have her card,' but the man said no . . . and quarreled with him. And he told the man, 'Look, this is a Senator.' I said, 'No, former Senator,' and he said, 'Madam, once a Senator, always a Senator.' I said, 'Thank you,' and kept quiet. In the process he gave me a paper and took my picture, and I was accredited" (30). Perry was admitted because of her political identity, not her maternal one. And although she was initially denied admittance, she did not have to insist, lobby, or demand participant status, especially since she was already on the roster as a political representative.

Once selected as interim head of state, Perry felt the gravity of being a woman in a position of great political power. She viewed this power as something in which all women should share. She recalled, "I felt the strength, the need, the will power to take it and move on. But not alone—I decided to first of all put it to prayer. Then, secondly, I mobilized the women and challenged them because I felt this challenge was not for Ruth Perry alone. It was for the women of Liberia and African women as a whole" (30). The challenge, to Perry, was to ensure peaceful elections. Drawing on her relationships to peace women, organizations, and networks, she mobilized Liberian women to share her objectives. She said, "I wanted unconditional peace for Liberia. . . . I projected myself as a true mother and a stabilizer" (31). To Perry the dwelling practices of a "true mother and stabilizer" strengthened relationships between Liberians, promoting Liberia as a dwelling place for women (and men) to belong.

Perry's selection and performance as interim head of state exposed the resistance and willingness of men to dwell with women in political places. Annie Saydee, president of the Rural Women's Association, reflected on Perry's national leadership: "Even though we were going all over to talk to people in the various counties, this southeastern part of the country was not included. Those four counties were out, and they never received food from anywhere because they say the road was blocked. So nobody traveled there until Ruth Perry got there. . . . She [found] a way for southeastern people to get something to eat" (31). Perry, much like the women who carved out roads between turfs, traveled to places that others could or would not go. When considered as a dwelling place, the nation became a place wherein women's dwelling practices forged literal (and lifesaving) pathways and relationships between Liberians. In this sense, dwelling practices enabled movement and flow, countering the notion that dwelling is about occupying or merely being in a place. Perry's dwelling practices, as well as those of other peace women, then, modeled a kind of belonging that challenged belonging as the occupation and territorialization of turfs across the nation.

Dwelling Inside and Outside Politics: The Second Civil War

Although Perry's leadership ensured that the elections of 1997 were peaceful, the results were highly suspect. General Charles Taylor was elected president with almost 100 percent of the vote. His presidency, then, was widely considered a sham and a thinly-veiled attempt to legitimize dictatorial leadership. The election catalyzed a wave of intensified warfare, violence, and displacement. In April 2003, for instance, one woman said, "Even as I speak, I can't give account of my three children. We can no longer sit and watch our children dying." Another displaced woman said, "I have not seen this child's father. . . . I was pregnant for her when I left Tubmanburg. But I have not seen her father. I am still running" (*LWP*, 47). By May 2003 many displaced persons headed for Monrovia, hoping to find basic human resources. At the time, LWI Secretary General Etweda Cooper said, "Monrovia does not have the infrastructure to accommodate the displaced that are coming. We don't have running water and electricity and basically the countryside is being captured, and therefore we will have problems with food coming to Monrovia" (47). Liberia, its villages and capital city, was almost uninhabitable, and yet the thing Liberians needed the most was a place to inhabit. As Gbowee put it, "The entire country was on the run, but there was nowhere left to go" (*MBOP*, 159).

It was in this context, as violence peaked in 2003, that peace women engaged in more militant dwelling practices such as silent peace marches and public prayer meetings. Between April and August 2003, they occupied an air field and places outside embassies and Monrovia City Hall, barricaded men inside peace talks, and threatened to strip bare. Through these more militant strategies, the women dwelled together with other women, made public and political places their homes, and asserted their belonging to a peaceful nation. The destabilization and temporary restabilization of what counted as a dwelling place or "home" was necessary as the destruction of homes and displacement of people escalated. Peace women engaged in what Rosenau described as "making the boundaries between home and away/ inside and outside both permeable and flexible."[54] Through dwelling practices such as sitting, praying, dancing, and marching, peace women asserted as their homes dwelling places such as fields, parking lots, streets, and conference hotels. The boundaries of these dwelling places were permeable insofar as women of all religions and classes could join, and many women could come and go and shuttle back and forth between sites of protest and their temporary homes (refugee camps for many). Boundaries were also flexible in that they expanded and contracted to accommodate the fluctuating numbers of women who dwelled together and the emergence of new dwelling places in light of almost-daily shifts in political exigencies.

Groups typically embrace militant strategies when they have exhausted more moderate ones. As an approach to social change, militancy is typically guided by the assumption that those in power must be held responsible for change and that protesters are willing to confront those in power without fear of consequence. As a particular set of strategies, militancy is context dependent and can take many different forms.[55] By 2002, for example, Liberian peace women had reached a breaking point where it seemed direct confrontation was a necessary next step to effect change. Most prominently, WIPNET's Liberian Mass Action for Peace brought together Christian and Muslim women, indigenous and Americo-Liberian women, women living on the streets and in the countryside, and women from displaced persons camps. A coalition of peace organizations, including MARWOPNET and LWI, followed Gbowee's lead as she and core leaders of WIPNET strategized and mobilized women in response to almost-daily changes in the political and violent wrangling over striking a peace accord.[56]

Gbowee and other peace women escalated to militant strategies that entailed public dwelling practices in which women dwelled together where they could literally and symbolically confront General Taylor, faction leaders, and other powerbrokers. To these ends, dwelling practices centered on disrupting political goings-on and confronting soldier and rebel leaders with masses of insistent and tireless women. These practices required women to mobilize, strategize, network, travel, and assemble so that they could present a united, unwavering force always in the faces of the men they blamed for the deaths of their children and the destruction of the nation. Through the relentless deployment of militant dwelling practices, peace women constituted public and political places as places where they belonged.

On April 1, 2003, Gbowee devised a new strategy. She had left her children and a paying job to volunteer full-time for WIPNET. Fed up with the war and its leaders, she called six other WIPNET leaders to her office. This meeting marked the beginning of their militant campaign. At first the campaign included broadcasting, planning, and assembling. On April 2, for example, they released a public statement over a Catholic radio station and in a local newspaper "condemning violence committed on all sides and making a single demand: 'The women of Liberia want peace now!'" (*MBOP*, 134). While directed to Taylor, the message drew hundreds of women to WIPNET's campaign offices in Monrovia. Within the campaigning, planning, and launching processes, these women dwelled together in the small spaces of empty apartments to strategize and make signs. A conflict between government and rebel soldiers at a nearby displaced persons camp also compelled victims of the conflict—women in muddy, torn clothing—to walk to Monrovia and join WIPNET's efforts. In response to the conflict, WIPNET planned a rally at City Hall, fully aware that Taylor had "banned street marches" (135). On April 11 at 8:00 a.m., as Gbowee recalls, hundreds of women, or "maybe as many as a thousand," arrived at the steps of City Hall. After many women spoke and testified to how the war had affected their lives, Gbowee addressed the crowd: "'In the past, we were silent,' I told the crowd. 'But after being killed, raped, dehumanized and infected with diseases, and watching our children and families destroyed, war has taught us that the future lies in saying *no* to violence and *yes* to peace! We will not relent until peace prevails!'"

Collectively, the crowd shouted "Peace! Peace!" WIPNET leaders gave Taylor three days to respond to their demands: declare a cease-fire, bring government and rebel leaders together to talk, and allow an intervention force into Liberia (135). When Taylor did not respond, they escalated yet again.

In the early hours of April 14, Gbowee and other WIPNET leaders walked to a large field off Tubman Boulevard by which Taylor drove to and from the Executive Mansion every day. Gbowee describes the scene: "As the sky got lighter, I looked around anxiously. For the protest to succeed, we needed at least a few hundred women. Finally, one group arrived. Then another. The sun rose. And then I heard the sound of diesel engines and up the road toward me came a line of buses. Mixed in there were trucks—trucks full of women" (137). More than two thousand women arrived, women of governmental agencies and NGOs, professors and college students, and women from displaced persons camps who walked for hours in ratty clothes. WIPNET organizers passed out white T-shirts to make sure all the women wore white, "to signify peace." Gbowee explains, "Liberian women love to dress up, but we'd come to the field completely bare of makeup and jewelry, in the kind of 'sackcloth and ashes' described in the Book of Esther, where the heroic queen stands up to save her people" (136). A few hours passed before Taylor's envoy approached the field. The women ignored the well-known fact that, when Taylor's envoy passed, "anyone on the road was expected to turn away or risk being shot" (137). In unison "the women rose, walked to the roadside and faced the president's convoy holding a huge banner: THE WOMEN OF LIBERIA WANT PEACE! NOW!" (137). Taylor's car slowed but did not stop. The women would call his bluff and over the next many months, dwell together in political and public places, inhabiting these places because they belonged to them, and they refused for these places to be anything but peaceful.

These rhetorical dwelling practices targeted the people and places of political power. After the three days of sitting together in the field, the women had not yet heard from Taylor and mobilized to stand in the parking lot in front of Parliament to deliver another three-day ultimatum. They returned to sit in the sandy, hot field to await a response from Taylor. Three days passed without word, so they returned to fill Parliament's parking lot again and ensured that legislators could not park (*LWP*, 46). The Speaker of the House stepped out to question them. When he asked Gbowee, "Why are you using these women for your personal interests?" Gbowee made clear LWI's political message: "If anyone is using anyone, it is *you!* You are all using the people of Liberia for your own selfish gains!" (*MBOP*, 138). Gbowee exposed the lie that the women's intent was merely "personal" and the work of the men was "political." Moreover, she positioned the Speaker, and implicitly, all other elected officials, in opposition to "the people of Liberia," the people who inhabited and belonged to Liberia. The women were the ones who sat in, who stood in, who belonged to, and who were "the people of Liberia."

The women's dwelling practices and places also sent another message: the women are united in their suffering together. To the Speaker of the House, Gbowee added, "We will continue to sit in the sun and in the rain until we hear from the president!" (138). In this instance Gbowee situated their dwelling places as "in the sun" and "in the rain." Indeed, days in the field meant sitting on hot sand in 90–100 degree heat for twelve hours a day (137). Gbowee recalls the sensation:

> Dawn to dusk in the heat. It's one thing to go about your business on a very hot day and another to sit, unmoving, while the sun bakes you. It was a kind of torture. I turned as black as I've ever been, and many of the women broke into rashes. But there was something compelling in the pain, too: your body was being beaten, but you were doing it for a reason. . . . From dawn to dusk in the rain. Liberia is one of the wettest countries on earth and the water comes down at you with the strength of a fireman's hose. We sat wretched as the flood sank into the field's sandy dirt. (142)

They stood and sat *in* heat, rain, and pain. Practicing dwelling as willful infliction of pain not only communicates a willingness endure suffering, but it also pushes against the notion of dwelling as inaction. Their suffering and refusal to seek comfort displayed an active, inexhaustible pushback against comfort and complacency with the status quo.

Their suffering also solidified a shared identity among the women as united in their battle for peace. On the rainy day at Parliament and on another day at the field, the women were offered shelter. Both times they refused: "'When a battle breaks out,' we explained, 'there's no time to grab an umbrella'" (138, 142). In another instance, when Gbowee and a handful of WIPNET leaders were invited inside the Executive Mansion to speak to Taylor, the women refused to sit. One woman addressed a guard: "When the bombs fall, we don't run carrying chairs. We are sharing everything our sisters go through" (140). To Gbowee attempts to accommodate the women were motivated out of "shame for their own inaction," and the women refused to let Taylor, legislators, and passersby see anything other than the

Figure 1   WIPNET members protest at the American Embassy in Monrovia.
Photo courtesy of Pewee Flomoku.

pain and suffering inflicted by the war and the pain and suffering they would endure for peace.

Dwelling together in suffering was just as much about presenting a united front to political elites as it was about forging an identity of women who belonged to each other. Gbowee said that through these practices, the women "had discovered a new source of power and strength: each other" (137). Throughout their months-long campaign, WIPNET facilitated a coalitional effort. On the field, women from Christian Women's Peace Initiative and Muslim Women for Peace led prayers, chants, and songs (139). Some women preached while others danced. In towns around Liberia, women organized sit-ins (*LWP*, 47). After days on the field, WIPNET leaders met in their offices and worked into the hours of the morning to make new placards, to design messages for the media, to discuss finances, and to figure out how to amass groups of women in strategic places (*MBOP*, 139). Meanwhile, women leaders from each of Liberia's nine political parties forged a coalition and reiterated WIPNET's demands for cease-fire, dialogue, and intervention. While these women leaders worked inside places reserved for political activity, WIPNET members worked outside such spaces. Working in concert, party and peace leaders redrew the boundaries of dwelling places, places where women united, demanded, and interrupted the work of political elites.

Shortly thereafter male faction leaders entered peace talks in Accra, Ghana. Talks went on for two and a half months, during which WIPNET leaders and other women intensified their dwelling practices—inside and outside places reserved for official political work. Only eight MARWOPNET women, including Perry and Leigh-Sherman, were accredited to attend and observe the talks (*LWP*, 9). While these women sat inside the talks, Gbowee rounded up "leaders of civil society and hundreds of women from a neighbouring refugee camp" to dwell in the spaces "on the perimeter" of the meeting hall.[57] According to a first-person account, "every day, between 150 and 200 refugee women arrived at the hotel where the talks were being held."[58] Gathering these women on the perimeter of the talks was strategic. After Gbowee refused an invitation to sit at the negotiation table, she explained that she supported the "elite" women of MARWOPNET who "represented the interests of all Liberian women," while WIPNET's role was to represent "our country's women in protest" (*MBOP*, 156). Gbowee sought to exploit the combined power of women to dwell inside *and* outside political spaces.

The most dramatic illustration of outside dwelling took place when women locked arms and blocked men from leaving the conference hall. One observer recalled, "On one occasion, when one received news of a relative being killed in Monrovia, the group of women responded by physically blockading the door to the delegates' meeting room for several hours, locking them in and refusing to let them leave (or even, as many remember, to use the toilet) until they came to agreements" (*LWP*, 13). Gbowee remembers that she and two hundred other women blocked the glass doors to the meeting room until the hallway became "hot and crowded with a sea of white T-shirts and black-lettered signs: BUTCHERS AND MURDERERS OF THE LIBERIAN PEOPLE—STOP!" (*MBOP*, 161). When the women weren't blocking doors, they filled the hallways, upheld "placards calling for an end to the violence, and sometimes confronted the faction leaders directly and forcefully" (*LWP*, 5, 12). In these instances the women inhabited the liminal spaces of the peace talks, threatening the men with their belonging. Like the hallways, these outer spaces are not meant for loitering or sitting. They are spaces for ingress and egress, movement and transition. For the women to practice dwelling as sitting in a liminal space intended for passing through, they demonstrated how dwelling practices function as a rhetoric of disruption. Indeed, the men could not leave the conference hall without facing or engaging with the women, as the women insisted that they inhabit the liminal spaces where men would pass through.

The women's dwelling practices insisted on their belonging to the peace talks and to a peaceful nation, particularly as they asserted their belonging as mothers to the men. Exhausted and impatient, the women exploited their maternal authority to threaten and shame the men. When security guards threatened to arrest the women for obstructing justice, Gbowee quipped, "I will make it very easy for you to arrest me. I'm going to strip naked" (*MBOP*, 161). One woman recalled the significance of Gbowee's threat: "For a son to see his mother's nakedness—it's considered a curse. And to do it in public! So the men were saying, 'we better do something because they're threatening to take their clothes off'" (*LWP*, 13). Gbowee exposed her legs. She explained, "In threatening to strip, I had summoned up a traditional power. In Africa, it's a terrible curse to see a married or elderly woman deliberately bare herself. If a mother is really, really upset with a child, she might take out her breast and slap it, and he's cursed. For this group of men to see a woman naked would be almost like a death sentence. Men are born through women's vaginas, and it's as if by exposing ourselves, we say, 'We now take back the life we gave you.' Fear passed through the hall" (*MBOP*, 162). In a Liberian context, these women—most of them married, widowed, or older mothers—threatened to curse the men if they did not reach an agreement. It worked. Immediately, men in the hall begged Gbowee to stop. General Abubakar of Ghana, the host and mediator of the peace talks, shamed the men and agreed to hear WIPNET leaders in private. He supported their demands for international media coverage and protection for remaining in the hallways for the remainder of the talks. In this case the peace women dwelled in the liminal spaces of politics, practiced obstruction, and exercised maternal power. In so doing, they dwelled in and belonged to the negotiations that would secure peace for Liberia. Moreover, unlike the more elite women of MARWOPNET, they insisted on dwelling in hallways to impress on the men inside negotiations that they posed a threat.

By the middle of August, all parties had signed a peace agreement. Over 2,500 women had been praying, singing, and dancing "on the side of the road, in sun and rain, every single day" for the previous three months.[59] Unsurprisingly, disarmament and ceasefire did not take place quickly. Demanding immediate implementation of the accord, peace women continued to dwell together in public places, asserting their belonging to the political processes of peacemaking. According to one account, "Women dressed in white t-shirts to symbolize peace marched on West African peace forces' headquarters in driving rain . . . pleading for faster deployment into Liberia's still-unsettled and starving interior. The roughly 100 women . . . waved rain-wilted signs with slogans urging *Total peace, not half peace*, *War everyday* and *Our sisters in Liberia are dying* . . . 'We want peace, no more war,' the women chanted" (*LWP*, 53).

Figure 2 WIPNET members sit in the football field on October 13, 2005, where Leymah Gbowee initiated the Mass Action for Peace two years earlier. They continued to sit after Sirleaf's election to protest ongoing violence against women. Photo courtesy of Paul Taggart, photojournalist (https://paultaggart.photoshelter .com, 2009).

Simultaneously in Accra, peace women of MARWOPNET and forty-five women's organizations came together to strategize. Meeting in the Golden Tulip Hotel, they drafted the Golden Tulip Declaration, which functioned as an agreement "to work toward the inclusion of all women within all existing and incoming Liberian Government . . . and within all structures to lead the post-conflict peace-building process" (51). Across multiple dwelling places and practices, the peace women militantly asserted their belonging to each other, to the political processes of peacemaking, and to a peaceful nation.

Conclusion: The Precarity and Possibilities of Denizenship

This case study illuminates how dwelling practices, as enactments of belonging to a place and to a nation, constitute denizenship as belonging for those denied it via formal citizenship. Likewise, these practices can transform places and nations from the homes or turfs of the violently oppressive into places and nations where the marginalized and the abused can assert their belonging. This case illustrated how dwelling can register in at least three ways. First, dwelling practices can take place within homes, traditionally conceived, toward multiple ends. Through meeting, consoling, and dialoguing, activists can exploit the way that civil warfare often destabilizes the romantic idea of home as a site of stability and security such that they can make the strange comfortable. They can welcome, listen to, and hold one another, and plan and sit together, if only for moments; they can also enter the homes of oppressors to listen to them and earn their trust. Altogether, dwelling practices within homes help transform the boundaries and meanings of "home" from sites of violation or threat into temporary sites of identification between activists, oppressors, and resistant sympathizers.

Second, activists can assert dwelling practices within the landscape of a nation to transform fiercely guarded turfs, destroyed infrastructure, and devastated countryside into a series of networked roads, paths, and relationships between activists, oppressors, and the helpless. As activists travel between multiple actors, they traverse the political and material contours of challenging terrain. Through walking, driving, carrying messages, and negotiating, activists can dwell with each other and oppressors within the nation-as-home. They can forge paths and relationships between and among multiple stakeholders, enabling flows of goods, resources, and information. In turn, activists can transform a contested political and material landscape into a site of productive relationships.

Third, activists can dwell within the places of peacemaking. Asserting their belonging to these places—hallways, conference rooms, registration tables—activists can transform peacemaking negotiations from sites where actors vie over political power and material resources into sites of healing and mediation. Through organizing, researching, raising funds, arriving, meeting, sitting, lobbying, speaking, and mourning with multiple actors, activists can assert their belonging not only to the places and processes of peacemaking but also to the kind of nation they wish to inhabit. Some activists escalate their dwelling practices to create sites of belonging, both inside and outside official sites of peacemaking and policymaking. Activists can enact militant dwelling through public speaking, blocking, marching, shuttling, threatening, praying, and singing. These dwelling practices assert their belonging to a peaceful nation where demands and voices aren't ancillary but central to nationbuilding and peacebuilding.

Through the dynamic deployment of these dwelling practices, the peace women of West Africa enacted denizenship as the means to survive and matter, when citizenship was no longer a viable mode of belonging. Their dwelling practices suggest that in nations and places that undergo violent challenges to what it means to be a citizen or to enact citizenship, *practicing* belonging can transform places considered "home"—places that may or may not have been sites of safe and secure belonging—into places where practicing together renegotiates and forges new relationships. Practicing together enacts dwelling together, which in turn can transform homes, roads, conference halls, and nations into temporary sites where denizens can belong.

Viewing the activism of peace women as the enactment of denizenship accounts for their work as the stuff of belonging, rather than the means to belonging. In that sense, this chapter has accounted for *how* disenfranchised women asserted *belonging to*. Denizenship, however, begs the question of *where* the disenfranchised belong. This case study simultaneously reifies and challenges the power of national and physical boundaries to define belonging. Denizens, politically and rhetorically, have a precarious relationship with the nation-state insofar as they are defined as *not citizens*, but they are *not citizens* with some degree of state-recognized permission to dwell within. From this perspective, denizens must belong *within* national boundaries. Yet because of their precarious position as *not citizens*, denizens often practice belonging to ethnic and religious enclaves, neighborhoods, and gathering places in ways that supersede their belonging to their host nation. When national and physical boundaries are challenged and violated à la regional conflict, denizens' precariousness simultaneously makes them more vulnerable and able to migrate across local, state, and regional boundaries. The peace women of Liberia and West Africa more broadly teach us that, in these dire contexts, if you take your dwelling practices with you, you might not only survive, but you might also transform your contexts into the places where you desire to belong.

This study also problematizes the idea of "home" as a site of dwelling practices and belonging, especially for women. In post-conflict West Africa, women and families sought to settle into homes, traditionally conceived. That said, for many women "home" is a far cry from the safe space theorized by Heidegger. In fact, reported acts of domestic violence have increased since the end of the second war in 2003. Studies argue that husbands are the biggest threat to the survival of women and children.[60] Survey data suggest that 70–73 percent of women are sexually assaulted by their husbands at home, not by strangers or soldiers. These reports include anecdotes from women about their husbands who spend money on girlfriends and leave their families to starve and threaten to beat their wives for trying to speak with them about their behavior. These reports directly confront the viability of speaking with husbands as a dwelling practice, as a strategy for belonging to "home," traditionally conceived. Yet these reports also spotlight how women gathered to share these stories of abuse, stories of how they engaged the state apparatus to report abuse, how the state failed them, how they feel hopeless, and how they desire business skills to survive. Thus, abused women may practice dwelling together—enacting belonging—to subvert the violently enforced boundaries of belonging to home.

To an extent this study of denizenship reaffirms the power of the nation-state, while it spotlights its vulnerability to undergo transformation. Women sought peace in their nations and recognized the power of national political elites to define and enable belonging. Amidst civil war, in the absence of a traditional state apparatus, women targeted political and military leaders of factions to plead their case. Through their dwelling practices, however, peace women asserted and insinuated themselves into the places and processes of decision-making such that they didn't just recognize and appeal to the power of men to define and enforce belonging; they transformed and became part of the places and processes of decision-making such that they wielded power to define and enforce belonging. One clear indication of this was that MARWOPNET functioned as one of the signatories to the Accra Accord, signed by all Liberian political parties and factions (*LWP*, 51).

In all, this study illustrates the empowering and disempowering potential of denizenship when defined as a set of dwelling practices. Considering that rates of domestic abuse and sexual assault continued to spike in the decade following the peace accord, it's clear that peace women and their dwelling practices alone cannot undo a culture that supports practices of male domination. To be sure, peace women did not stop their peacemaking work once a peace accord was reached. They transitioned to the work of peace building, including volunteering, organizing, and registering women to vote throughout Ellen Johnson Sirleaf's presidential campaign. Sirleaf's successful election (and reelection), I argue, can be attributed in great part to the campaign work of peace women and to their dwelling practices, which made visible the work and belonging of women to homes, the nation, and politics. How Sirleaf built on the work of peace women to appeal to Liberian women, to respond to gendered concerns in national and local politics, and to enable Liberian women and girls to learn, lead, legislate, and work is addressed in the next chapter.

2

BELONGING AS COSMOPOLITANISM:
ELLEN JOHNSON SIRLEAF'S NEW NATIONALISM

On January 16, 2006, Liberians crowded the streets of Monrovia and the grounds of the Capitol Building to celebrate the dawn of a new national era. Prior to the celebration, hundreds of Liberians labored over the war-ravaged grounds, filling and painting over bullet holes, removing waist-high piles of debris, and constructing a stage. Neat rows of chairs were reserved for honorable guests, including eight African presidents and representatives from China, Egypt, France, and Finland, as well as US First Lady Laura Bush and Secretary of State Condoleezza Rice. As guests arrived streamers of red, white, and blue waved amidst jubilant citizens who sang, danced, drummed, and cheered in the name of the woman christened "The Iron Lady of Liberia," "Queen of Africa," and, affectionately, "Ma Ellen." All gathered to witness the inauguration of Liberia's first democratically elected president, Ellen Johnson Sirleaf.

Sirleaf attracted worldwide attention as the first woman president of an African nation. To many Liberians Sirleaf's election meant the end of a century and a half of single-party rule and more crucially, the end of two civil wars that spanned fourteen years. Between 1989 and 2003, Liberians saw the murder of 270,000 of its three million citizens, the displacement of one million citizens, the rise of a 90 percent unemployment rate, a debt of $3.7 billion, and near-total destruction of all infrastructure that left Liberians without running water and electricity. During the wars, factions conscripted as soldiers more than fifteen thousand boys, who were drugged and forced to turn on their own family members.[1] Rebel camps took women and girls as slave wives. Such abuses spurred on massive national and regional women's pro-peace protests that helped broker a ceasefire and mobilized Liberian women to register and vote for Sirleaf.

Thus, as Sirleaf approached the podium to take the presidential oath, she faced a hopeful, yet fragile nation. Staring from the front row were her former presidential opponents, vestiges of a corrupt "old boys club" of politics, whose attendance signaled a tentative commitment to democratic governance. Watching from the crowds were former soldiers and rebels, many of whom had no idea what it meant to live without war. Also watching were Liberian women and girls, many of whom imagined for the first time a secure and peaceful existence. Also watching were the peace women who had helped elect Sirleaf and who had forged belonging as denizenship in response to how civil warfare foreclosed belonging as national citizenship. In this moment and throughout her two presidential terms, Sirleaf's rhetoric needed to reimagine what it meant to belong to a nation and how Liberians could go about the business of belonging.

This was an especially important rhetorical task so that women and girls, whose social, political, and economic lives had always been dominated by men, could imagine belonging as valued citizens. While thousands of women participated in peace activism throughout the civil wars, most of Liberia's 1.5 million women did not, either because they were beset with the mere struggle to survive or because the risk of retribution was too great. Whether or not they forged belonging as denizens, Liberian women and girls did not belong to Liberia as fully enfranchised national citizens. Sirleaf was aware that finding a way for women and girls to belong as citizens required symbolic and structural change. In her memoir she said that, as president, she had a mandate to create "a real sense of national identity" as well as to fix "the roads and the power and the schools and the industries that create jobs."[2]

Sirleaf's commitment to women was so strong that, at the end of her historic inaugural address delivered before Liberians and African dignitaries and to champions of women's rights and democracy all over the world, she said:

> Until a few decades ago, Liberian women endured the injustice of being treated as second-class citizens. During the years of our civil war, they bore the brunt of inhumanity and terror. They were conscripted into war, gang raped at will, forced into domestic slavery. . . .
>
> My Administration shall thus endeavor to give Liberian women prominence in all affairs of our country. My Administration shall empower Liberian women in all areas of our national life. We will support and increase the writ of laws that restore their dignities and deal drastically with crimes that dehumanize them. . . . We shall encourage families to educate all children, particularly the girl child. We shall also try to provide economic programs that enable Liberian women to assume their proper place in our economic revitalization process.[3]

Unequivocally, Sirleaf was committed to undoing a "second-class citizen" status for women, to treating them as humans, and to making them a central part of "national life." She was fiercely dedicated to symbolic and material change to social, political, and economic norms that devalued their bodies and their potential to learn, lead, and work. How would Sirleaf's international, national, and policymaking rhetorics craft an identity for the women and girls of a postconflict nation? That is, what norms, rights, and resources would her presidential rhetoric promote? In short, how would her rhetoric craft belonging for women *as citizens*?

This chapter is focused on answering those questions in terms of Liberian women and girls, especially considering that their relationship to the nation-state was always defined in the negative: they were *not* men, and therefore any rights, privileges, education, property, and/or political clout they earned was earned in spite of being women. While men, too, suffered psychological and physical abuse throughout the nation's history of single-party rule and civil warfare, they always belonged to the nation-state with greater state-recognized and social power than women. Moreover, Sirleaf is an internationally recognized women's rights advocate who made specific promises to empower Liberian women and girls. Previously, the UN commissioned her to study how war affects women's lives all over the world. She also suffered the violence of war firsthand when soldiers abducted her, forced her to cook and clean, imprisoned her, and threatened to rape her. This chapter, then, seeks to understand her rhetoric for *what* it enabled women to do and *how* it changed what it meant to belong to a nation.

I argue that Sirleaf reimagined belonging for Liberian women and girls as national cosmopolitans whose actions as educated leaders, political leaders, and marketing entrepreneurs contributed to the betterment of the nation, the West African region, and the world. To (re)orient Liberian women and girls to the nation-state, an apparatus that had long abused and ignored them, she crafted a belonging for them that included and superseded belonging to the nation. With the norms she promoted in the international arena to audiences around the world, the values she rehearsed to audiences in the region and nation, and the policies she helped implement, Sirleaf created a belonging for women not only as national citizens but also as citizens whose natural abilities necessitated a redefinition of national citizenship.

The following explains why Sirleaf's rhetoric is an ideal case study for examining belonging as national cosmopolitanism, how Liberia's postwar moment and Sirleaf's rhetorical leadership enabled the crafting of a cosmopolitan rhetoric, and how she deployed this rhetoric of belonging through a three-part strategy.

National Cosmopolitanism

As the pressures and effects of globalization intensified throughout the 1990s and the first decade of the 2000s, political theorists turned to the concept of cosmopolitanism as a potential antidote to the human costs of a "free" market. Martha Nussbaum, for example, considered cosmopolitanism as a moral imperative to "make all human beings part of our community of dialogue and concern."[4] Nussbaum placed this moral and ethical responsibility on the individual to negotiate their "strong duties to humanity" with devotion to the "particular people and places we love."[5] Likewise, "the cosmopolitan patriot[s]," as Kwame Anthony Appiah described them, take it as a "citizen's responsibility" to care for their home country, enjoy the different peoples and places of the world, and at the same time, deplore the forces of involuntary "migration, nomadism, and diaspora."[6]

Critics of this strain of thought argued that cosmopolitanism urged a dis-identification with one's national community or at least a primary identification with a global community. To Amy Gutman, for example, dis-identification was impractical. She asks, in a world where the nation-state is the primary agent of defining citizenship rights and practices, how would "global citizens" be enabled to act on a moral obligation to the whole of humanity?[7] In response, some scholars argue that the increasingly centralized power of supranational organizations, such as the UN, could be exploited to normalize cosmopolitan values into its policies. Luis Cabrera, for example, argues for "a defensible system of global institutions" to protect and enable "global citizens" in a quest for a better humanity.[8] More explicitly, Barbara Arneil calls on "those that currently have power in the international system," such as the World Health Organization, "to partake in transformative change in order to embrace a different kind of world."[9] To her this would mean the implementation of policies that would protect the rights of global citizens to ameliorate poverty, disease, and gender injustice.[10]

And still many scholars maintain that the normalizing and legal power of the nation-state and national community is not going away anytime soon. Indeed, when the UN passes a mandatory resolution, member states must implement them at the level of the nation-state. Seyla Benhabib, for example, argues that practicing cosmopolitanism in our everyday lives must begin with the nation-state's adoption of universally accepted cosmopolitan values that, once codified, could govern relationships between individuals in local circumstances.[11] Ulrich Beck similarly argues for "universal procedural norms" to be implemented at the national level that would, in turn, enable what he calls "realistic cosmopolitanism."[12] This brand of cosmopolitanism, he argues, fuses nationally adopted cosmopolitan values with local expression: "Cosmopolitan realism does not negate nationalism but presupposes it and transforms it into a cosmopolitan nationalism."[13]

Legislating and normalizing cosmopolitanism at the level of the nation-state is only part of the solution, according to rhetorician Kathleen Glenister Roberts. She reminds us that a study of cosmopolitanism "is impossible without attention to the everyday practices—discursive and otherwise—of diverse groups."[14] Roberts and other communication scholars pair cosmopolitanism with provinciality such that one's "everyday practices" in their local community sustain a moral obligation toward all of humanity—a moral obligation that would likewise drive national policy changes that would allow for the practice of cosmopolitanism in the local.[15] Thus, to scholars of politics and rhetoric, cosmopolitan values and practices constitute mutually-reinforcing relationships between the global, national, and local. Globally, cosmopolitan values circulate and direct nation-states to codify them, such that locally, citizen actors practice cosmopolitanism in ways that positively impact local, national, regional, and global communities. In turn, these citizens fashion cosmopolitanism as an ideal mode of national citizen engagement.

And yet, while scholars have advocated for the practice of national cosmopolitanism in "real-lived communities," they have stopped short of tracking *how* cosmopolitan values could become universalized in global arenas and enabled in national arenas, *what* local practices enacted national cosmopolitan values, and *how* the enactment of these practices fashioned a national cosmopolitan citizen ideal.[16] In fact, while the exigencies of enabling cosmopolitan citizenship practices continue to escalate, much of this scholarly conversation has died down since the late 2000s.[17] In the field of rhetorical studies with an abundance of scholarship on the violent exclusions and emancipatory functions of citizenship discourses, studies of cosmopolitan values and practices would complement and extend conversations that seek to connect universal norms, national policy, and local enactments of citizenship.[18] No doubt, scholarship that examines what it means to be a citizen in a world where national boundaries are increasingly porous and yet strictly enforced has made significant headway on exposing the rhetorical processes that perform both oppressive and liberatory functions.[19] That said, these studies tend to focus on the discourses of national institutions (presidential, legislative, or judicial) and/or social movements that agitate for national policy change. Furthermore, as Robert Asen reminds us, such studies have overwhelmingly focused on how discourses created, challenged, or rewrote *what* it means to be a citizen (or not) of a particular nation-state.[20]

This chapter seeks to expose the rhetorical processes that enable and constrain cosmopolitan practices as concrete steps toward a more emancipated humanity. I aim to pick up where political theory and rhetorical studies leave off to examine how presidential policy rhetoric helped normalize cosmopolitan values in the global arena, codified and enabled the expression of cosmopolitan values in the national arena, and ultimately transformed what and how citizenship counts. By "cosmopolitan values" I mean the concern and care for humankind, a composite of locally, nationally, and globally interrelated communities. By "cosmopolitan practices" I mean the everyday citizen acts that contribute to the well-being of national, regional, and/or global communities and, in turn, reshape what it means to be a national citizen. I demonstrate how belonging can be reimagined at the level of the nation-state. Reimagining belonging simultaneously engages and subverts what it means to be a citizen in the eyes of the nation-state and, in turn, enables women to practice belonging as ideal constituents of the nation, the region, and the world.

I take up Ellen Johnson Sirleaf's policy rhetoric as an exemplar of discourses that promoted cosmopolitan values to global audiences, extended cosmopolitan citizenship practices at the level of the nation-state, and in turn transformed national citizenship into cosmopolitan citizenship. Specifically, as the first democratically elected president of Liberia, Sirleaf enacted the rhetorical leadership necessary to universalize cosmopolitan values around the world, enable Liberian women to participate as citizen actors through cosmopolitan practices and, in turn, fashion a national brand of cosmopolitan citizenship that sought to improve national, regional, and global communities. In effect, Sirleaf regendered citizenship such that women's social, political, and economic citizenship practices constituted not only *what it meant* to belong but also *how* to belong.

To make these arguments, I examine Sirleaf's autobiography and public addresses from her first inaugural address through her last speech of 2013. Specifically, I first track how she enacted the rhetorical leadership necessary to universalize cosmopolitan norms in global, regional, and national arenas, noting the organizations and conferences she addressed and her advocacy of women's rights as a global mainstay. Second, I note the resources that

Sirleaf's policies and initiatives made available to women and how, to Sirleaf, they positioned Liberian women as national citizens whose social, political, and economic leadership would transform national, regional, and global communities. Third, I highlight how Sirleaf envisioned these women as fashioning cosmopolitan citizenship as the new norm of citizenship engagement, wherein local practice is part and parcel to national, regional, and global change.

The following offers a biographical and contextual sketch of Sirleaf and her rhetorical situation, emphasizing the constraints and opportunities for Sirleaf to craft cosmopolitan citizenship ideals and practices. Then an analysis exposes how Sirleaf's three-part rhetorical strategy normalized, enabled, and transformed citizenship as educated rhetorical action, political leadership, and marketing and entrepreneurialism. While all of these practices share educational, political, and economic dimensions, they are discussed thematically based on the goals of particular policies and initiatives. Finally, the conclusion considers how, altogether, Sirleaf's cosmopolitan rhetorical leadership helped normalize values, enable practices, and transform meaning for a previously disenfranchised group and how it points to the necessity for a feminist perspective on the emancipatory potential of cosmopolitanism rhetoric.

Sirleaf's Cosmopolitan Leadership and Situation

Sirleaf's rhetorical situation demanded that she reinvent national belonging, especially since Liberia had been led by single-party rule for most of its existence and more recently by brutal dictatorship. The civil wars are considered the result of long-standing tensions along race, class, and gender lines. Since 1822, when freed American slaves began to populate the area, what became known as Liberia was culturally and politically tied to the United States.[21] In fact, the "returned" slaves reproduced the United States's racial hierarchy and formed an elite social class referred to as "settlers" or Americo-Liberians.[22] Assuming superiority, Americo-Liberians enslaved and politically suppressed Liberia's indigenous groups for more than one hundred years.[23] Driven by this racial and political divide, a military coup in 1980 sparked decades of violence and civil warfare widely attributed to the unchecked power of male dictators, politicians, soldiers, and rebels.[24] Indeed, Liberian women and girls suffered extraordinary physical and psychological abuses, with three out of every four raped or sexually assaulted.[25]

Thus, Condoleezza Rice and Laura Bush's attendance at Sirleaf's inauguration signaled the United States's approval and support of Liberia's new democracy and of Sirleaf's ability to upend male domination and corruption.

Sirleaf's life experiences with Liberia's culture of male domination shaped her ethos as a woman unafraid to face resistance to change. Culturally and perhaps physically, Sirleaf can be "read" as Americo-Liberian, although her heritage is indigenous to Liberia and Europe. Each of her parents was fostered by a settler family at a young age, educated, and acclimated to Western culture. Her mother was half-native and half-German, providing for Sirleaf what Liberians call a "red" skin tone that indicated settler status. As a child she was teased for her light skin. She recalled, "They said I was too light to be a real African and called me Red Pumpkin, a name that hurt me to the bottom of my soul. Many days after school I cried my way home. Many nights I went to bed praying to God to let me wake up black" (*TCWBG*, 27). Despite how she appeared, her nonsettler status would eventually help her identify with Liberia's indigenous people.

Her father was the first native Liberian to hold a seat in Liberia's national legislature, although his political life was short-lived when he suffered a stroke. Because her father could no longer provide for the family, Sirleaf gave up hope of attending college and married at age seventeen. She had four children in rapid succession and soon found herself, as she said, "mothering my children and working a series of low-paying dead-end jobs that were taking me nowhere fast" (33). When her husband received a scholarship to study at the University of Wisconsin at Madison, she and her mother scrambled to find her a scholarship so that she could attend as well. After earning a degree in business, she returned to Liberia and eventually separated from her husband, an abusive alcoholic who had threatened her at gunpoint many times (38–42).

Sirleaf followed in her father's footsteps and took up a career in national politics. In the 1970s, Sirleaf served as the president's minister of finance and after Samuel Doe's takeover, was coerced to serve the new dictator in different advisory capacities. Still, she was free to work and travel. On a trip to Philadelphia to deliver a speech to the Union of Liberian Associations in the Americas, she publicly referred to Doe and his administrators as "idiots." Unafraid, she returned to Monrovia where Doe's handlers swiftly brought her back to the Executive Mansion. Doe and "several of his generals and top ministers" questioned and harassed her about the speech. She said, "I did not deny it; there was no point in doing so. . . . In their fury the men in the room began to taunt, curse, and berate me" (123–24). They accused her of plotting Doe's assassination, and she was placed under house arrest and then imprisoned for almost nine months. Accused of treason, Sirleaf described the days of her military tribunal: "Every day the soldiers would come to my cell at Monrovia's Central Prison to escort me to court on foot. It was during this time that I really became a kind of folk hero. The crowds would line the streets as I walked to my trial, surrounded by policemen. The atmosphere was far from menacing; some days it was almost festive, in fact" (129). Sirleaf was sentenced to ten years of hard labor in "a notorious rural prison in Liberia, a prison from which people did not return" (130). Before ever being transported to the prison, Sirleaf was granted clemency, an act many attributed to growing international pressure on Doe (131).

Soon after, Sirleaf accepted the vice-presidential nomination for the Liberian Action Party. While exit polls showed that her party's presidential nominee won the election with a clear majority, Doe's "Special Elections Commission" declared him the winner of the election. Sirleaf nonetheless won her county's Senate seat. Aware that her international reputation would have helped bolster the credibility of Liberia's new "democratic" government, she refused to take her seat in the Senate, a move that would soon come back to haunt her (135–38).

Approximately one year later, in November, a failed attempt to overthrow Doe threw him and his men "on a rampage, ready to wreak revenge on anyone" (140). Within hours, soldiers showed up at Sirleaf's home, "wild and drunk," "shooting wildly and randomly in the air" (141). To protect her mother from certain death, Sirleaf surrendered. From there Doe's soldiers took her to a camp, taunted and terrorized her, and shoved her into a tiny cell (143–45). That night, when a guard threatened to rape her, another guard intervened. He identified as Gola, the same indigenous group that Sirleaf's father belonged to. He asked her to prove her Gola lineage, and after she spoke a few words in Gola, he promised to protect her for the night (146).

In the morning a few of Doe's high-ranking soldiers attempted to persuade Sirleaf to take her legislative seat. Still, she refused. In response, the soldiers forced her to cook and clean for them. She remembered, "The soldiers wanted to humiliate me, to put me in my place. I knew I would have to bear whatever they came up with" (148). Shortly thereafter, Sirleaf was rounded up to be taken to Doe himself. Sirleaf remembered the dread of that Jeep ride: "I knew that if I were taken before Doe, the order would be immediate execution" (149). Fortunately, Doe's head of the Executive Mansion guard intervened before the soldiers brought Sirleaf to Doe. He ordered the soldiers not to harm her and instead to take her to prison (150). Sirleaf performed hard labor there until July of the next year, when Doe buckled under international pressure and released her and many other political prisoners. Sirleaf and the other freed prisoners rode on the back of a truck: "As it pulled out into the street, the crowds materialized and lined the sidewalks, cheering us on. Once again, we had become folk heroes to a people tired of governmental oppression and wrongdoing" (153). The crowds followed the truck until the prisoners were unloaded and began an impromptu rally. Sirleaf continued, "Someone brought a small table out into the street and I climbed on top of it, raising my fist in a powerful salute. . . . 'Freedom!' I cried. 'Freedom!' the crowd roared back" (153). Eventually, Doe was ousted by Charles Taylor, with whom Sirleaf attempted to work on implementing democracy, but on the brink of another civil war, Sirleaf left Liberia until a peace accord was reached in 2003.

Sirleaf's tumultuous involvement in national politics was punctuated by her career in transnational finance and global governance. She worked for corporations such as World Bank, Citibank, and Equator Bank. Moreover, she served in regional and supranational leadership roles in the UN as Assistant Secretary General of African Affairs for the UN Development Program, as an investigator of the Rwandan genocide, and a commissioner for the UN Development Fund for Women to investigate the effect of conflict on women around the world. Sirleaf's work in global and regional governance resonated with the women's regional peace movement to end civil warfare in West Africa.[26] Through a web of regional networks, grassroots leaders led seminars on mediation, provided counseling for survivors of sexual assault, and facilitated multiple peace talks between faction leaders. Eventually Liberian faction leaders signed a peace treaty, a feat attributed in great part to the women protesters. Thus, when Sirleaf decided to run for president in 2004, she had the full-throated support of many Liberian women who were reported to have boosted female voter registration to almost 50 percent.[27]

In sum, Sirleaf's upbringing, education, imprisonments, and career played key roles in shaping her cosmopolitan orientation to politics and women's rights—insofar as national politics could not be separated from regional and supranational politics. Sirleaf's ethos as a survivor of imprisonment, as an activist who spoke truth to power throughout her career, and as a woman personally familiar with the politics and costs of male domination and genocidal warfare constructed her as a leader with the strength to lead the new democracy. Upon her election, then, Liberians looked to see how the new president would transform a war-torn nation into a functioning democracy in which women and girls participated as fully enfranchised citizens.

The following analysis tracks Sirleaf's three-part strategy of normalizing gender policy, enabling rhetorical actors and practices, and transforming national citizenship into national cosmopolitanism.

Educated Rhetorical Action as Cosmopolitan Practice

In most theories of cosmopolitan citizenship, education is key toward understanding how national belonging is interlocked with regional and global belonging. Nussbaum's touchstone essay "For Love of Country" advocates that school curricula promote a moral obligation toward communities that include but also exceed one's national community.[28] Gutman adds, "Publicly subsidized schooling should teach students the rights and responsibilities of democratic citizenship," which is not moral allegiance to any community but "to justice—to doing what is right."[29] To her such an education significantly enables citizens to advocate and deliberate on behalf of "human beings throughout the world" who "are entitled to be treated as equals."[30] Recently, rhetorician Jay P. Childers demonstrated that, in a First World context, high school students developed cosmopolitan perspectives because they were increasingly able to identify with others as part of a shared global community.[31] Whether motivated by a commitment to community or to justice, cosmopolitan education ideally enables particular practices beneficial to national and global communities, including the act of speaking out against the unequal treatment of others. What's missing from this conversation, however, is an examination of *how* these values can become globally normalized and nationally codified so that students can develop and practice these cosmopolitan values in their local communities.

Sirleaf's educational and antirape initiatives demonstrate how a national leader can promote cosmopolitan values in the global arena, codify them in the national arena, and transform national citizenship. She did so through interrelated policy goals: to provide women and girls with an education and to protect them from sexual assault. Ideally, if women and girls were educated and free from the threat of sexual control, then they could access the resources they needed to speak out against the patrilineal practices of local, national, and global communities. Sirleaf's three-part rhetorical strategy first promoted girls' education and freedom from assault as shared values across supranational, national, and private organizations, all of which provided resources for Liberia's education initiatives. Second, Sirleaf argued that these resources enabled women as rhetorical actors to challenge patrilineal practices and in turn, undo such practices in multiple geopolitical arenas. Last, Sirleaf worked to normalize antipatrilineal rhetorical practice as a new mode of citizenship engagement.

First, it's important to understand the tight link between education and sexual freedom for Liberian women. Across indigenous groups and to different extents, women and girls were treated by men as powerful commodities. According to Veronika Fuest, "Powerful men accumulated women and controlled and redistributed women's sexual and reproductive services to establish political alliances and to win clients."[32] To these ends, fathers negotiated their daughters' bride wealth and virginity for socio-political power.[33] For indigenous women who could earn their own money, they were to use it to educate their daughters. These girls could venture into a more urban life as independent women but were often perceived as promiscuous "public" women.[34] If an educated indigenous girl became pregnant before marriage, she was thought to bring shame on her family and was relegated to becoming a poor "market woman," dependent on her father or husband for money.[35] For Americo-Liberian women, education was always valued as part of a more civilized and Western identity.[36] That said, throughout the wars, displacement and destruction precluded most girls from going to school. By the end of the civil wars, infrastructural and economic devastation coupled with women's forced sexual relations shaped a social scene that constrained women's educational opportunities and in turn, their identities as independent women, free from sexual control.[37]

From within these constraints, Sirleaf sought to enable Liberian women and girls as educated rhetorical actors, empowered to lead their communities and stem the tide of patrilineal abuse. She began by normalizing the values of women's education and women's protection from violence to international and national audiences. In 2006, for example, she addressed a meeting of the European Commission in Brussels, Belgium, and called for special programs that educate "the girl child and sensitize people to the evil of gender based violence."[38] Likewise, at a panel discussion hosted by the Clinton Global Institute in New York, Sirleaf stressed the "need to keep girls in school long enough so that they are not diverted into early marriage" and "to introduce in our educational systems the need for the protection of women, the role women play in our society; and to have the instruments and laws that will protect women."[39] The following year, Sirleaf reiterated these values to her national legislature after the passage of the 2011 Education Reform Act. The Act ensured that school was free through the ninth grade, which to Sirleaf was especially significant for "the girls, who have been falling behind because they've been dropping out right after primary school and all of us need to put an effort into it to stop teenage pregnancy, to stop the assault on our young girls."[40] As Sirleaf made explicit the link between school and sexual freedom, she aimed to normalize the value of free, educated girls in both the national and international arenas.

Sirleaf was particularly vehement about upholding and strengthening national and international antirape measures. Prominently, Sirleaf concluded her inauguration speech with the following declaration: "We will enforce without fear or favor the law against rape recently passed by the National Transitional Legislature."[41] The following year she addressed an audience of women world leaders, including Michelle Bachelet, president of Chile, and Tarja Halonen, president of Finland, on the importance of normalizing antirape policy in the global arena. She said, "Much more remains to be done if we, collectively, as nations, as governments, as civil society, as leaders are to succeed in discouraging and subsequently eliminating impunity against gender based violence."[42] Specifically, she called for "international laws and sanctions," "international efforts," and "international support."[43]

Sirleaf demonstrated how these values could shape national policy. Early in her first presidency, in 2008, she organized her Ministry of Gender and Development to establish Criminal Court E, which, as she said to her legislature, deals "exclusively with gender-based violence and the unacceptable high level of rape cases stemming from the violation of young girls."[44] The court not only provided infrastructural and bureaucratic support for victims of sexual assault, but its creation also performed a rhetorical function. To Sirleaf the court worked "to clearly articulate to the Liberian public that violence against women and girls will be treated with severe legal action."[45] After the court's establishment, Sirleaf addressed a UN meeting in Brazil and used the court as an example of how a nation-state can implement antirape measures.[46] In so doing she continued to normalize the importance of providing education and protection for young girls.

Sirleaf's promotion and implementation of these values were also manifested in educational programs and funds that enabled Liberian women and girls to assert themselves as rhetorical actors in local communities. She organized and addressed multiple actors, including her Ministry of Gender and Development and partners of nationally and regionally targeted private funds, including the Liberian Education Trust, the Sirleaf Market Women's Fund, and the African Women Development Fund (AWDF). Together these actors raised more than $6 million, which by 2010 had provided 3,500 scholarships for girls and literacy training for 3,500 women and had constructed

Figure 3   On January 15, 2013, President Ellen Johnson Sirleaf poses with US Secretary of State Hillary Clinton at the US Department of State. Photo: US Department of State.

twenty-eight schools.[47] Sirleaf linked these newly available resources and practices to the well-being of the nation. To an audience of world leaders in 2008, for example, she asserted, "When you educate a girl, you educate a nation. This is all part of our drive to 'change minds and change attitudes' about gender constructs."[48] To Sirleaf educating a girl meant educating the nation, which positioned Liberian girls as *the* national citizenry. It also invoked the notion that women and girls are the cultural and biological reproducers of the nation, responsible for educating their children and the children of their villages and communities. Taking it a step further, these programs enabled women and girls to teach and enact shifting gender ideals.

Sirleaf argued that these policies fashioned women and girls as rhetorical actors whose rhetorical practices would help undo patrilineality in Liberia and beyond. For example, Sirleaf argued that educated girls would stem child marriages and female circumcision. These rhetorical actors would "educate [their] families and communities on the evils inherent in such 'traditional' and 'cultural' practices" and "inculcate the practice of speaking out publicly against especially cases of rape and forced marriages."[49] Coupled with the antirape measures, women and girls could not only speak out against patrilineal practices, but they could also report instances of abuse without fear of retaliation. The new laws provided "effective complaint, counseling and monitoring mechanisms" as well as "guarantees of confidentiality."[50] Thus, women were enabled as rhetorical change agents in their local communities so that they could help shift what it meant to be a girl or a woman in Liberia.

In sum, Sirleaf's rhetorical strategies pushed back against how citizenship is practiced in Liberia and within the global arena. Normalizing education for women and women's protection from rape for national and global audiences casted acts such as going to school, educating communities, and accusing perpetrators of rape as ideal citizenship practices. These practices, while codified and enabled at the level of the nation-state, altered national citizenship engagement away from bargaining with the bodies of women and girls for power and from shaming independent women as promiscuous. Indeed, as more women and girls pursued an education, they fashioned speaking out against gender oppression as cosmopolitan citizen practice, beneficial to local, national, and global communities.

Political Leadership as Cosmopolitan Practice

To many theorists of cosmopolitanism, cosmopolitan practices and actors need to be enabled and supported through local, national, and global governance. To Benhabib these practices are premised on norms shared in the global arena. She argues, "[Cosmopolitanism is] the emergence of norms that ought to govern relations among individuals in a global civil society. These norms are neither merely moral nor just legal. They may be best characterized as framing the 'morality of the law,' but in a global rather than a domestic context."[51] Cabrera agrees that an individual can only get so far in effecting cosmopolitan change. His approach "views institutions as vital for the protection of human rights" and for the definition of "global human duties" to all human beings.[52] Thus legal or policy change in global governance is driven by and/or reflects changes in a global morality to protect others as global citizens. What's missing from these accounts is an explanation of how these institutional shifts take place. A rhetorical perspective of policy change often focuses on members of governing bodies as rhetorical actors who deliberate and contest policies that, upon passage, ideally reflect shared norms of governance among a majority of the governing body as well as the polity it represents.[53] In turn, such policies enable citizens to act in ways that reify these norms. Sirleaf's approach to ensuring positive policy change for women began with getting women into legislative bodies so they could assert themselves as rhetorical actors and shape policy. Her assumption was that, once women achieved critical mass in national, regional, and/or global governing bodies, women's rights policies could more readily be passed. To this end, Sirleaf first promoted the value of women's leadership to national and supranational audiences, working to collect resources for quota programs and women's political campaigns. Second, she argued that leadership enabled women to practice their natural collaborative leadership skills that would transform politics in local, national, and global arenas. Last, she normalized women's supranational and national leadership and the mainstreaming of national gender policies as ideal cosmopolitan citizenship practice.

First, it's important to understand the supranational, regional, and national political contexts in which Sirleaf promoted women's leadership. Women in Liberia have asserted political agency since before colonial times. Among natives, women were typically considered inferior to men, but women chiefs and councils of female elders could veto decisions of male leaders and wield control through relationships to powerful men.[54] In the early to mid-twentieth century, Liberia saw Americo-Liberian women in prominent administrative and political posts, including dean of Liberia College, minister of the State Department, and representatives in Liberia's National Legislature.[55] After the first civil war, a woman—Ruth Perry—led as interim head of state for two years. Across Africa, Sirleaf's election was in step with many women's elections to political offices. To date, Sub-Saharan African women hold 21.9 percent of the seats in their nation's legislative assemblies, a number 6.3 percent higher than it was ten years ago.[56] Also, since Sirleaf's election, six African women have served as prime minister or president on an interim or full-term basis.[57]

African women's regional leadership helped shape historic supranational policy. In 1995 at the UN's Fourth World Conference on Women, a delegation of African women confronted multiple heads of state about women's critical roles in conflict and peacekeeping.[58] Months later the UN Security Council passed Resolution UN Security Council Resolution (UNSCR) 1325, which ensured women's roles in peacekeeping missions and required protection of women against sexual assault.[59] Later Sirleaf was tasked with conducting an in-depth study on the effect of conflict on women and making specific recommendations to the security council on how to implement UNSCR 1325. As the result of heart-wrenching interviews with women across the globe, this study recommended that UN member states include women as policymakers. Sirleaf's role in implementing UNSCR 1325 shaped her view of women as grassroots change agents of supranational and national policy.

To enable women as political leaders, Sirleaf first promoted and helped normalize the value of women as policymakers to international and national audiences. Specifically, she promoted "gender mainstreaming," or the argument that a certain percentage of women in governing bodies ensured positive policy change for women (*LWP*, 23).[60] For example, at an UN leadership retreat in Torino, Italy, she insisted that nations adopt the UN's 30 percent quota of women in legislative bodies.[61] Likewise, at a regional meeting in Accra, Ghana, she urged heads of state to "develop rosters of viable female candidates to participate fully in the political arena; encourage women to register to vote and educate them about the electoral processes; teach female aspirants how to run effective campaigns; and enhance their leadership capacity."[62] To Sirleaf quantitative change meant qualitative change. At a World Leaders Panel Discussion in New York, Sirleaf made it clear that democracy is not possible without women's political leadership. She argued that "women's access in participatory institutions at the local, national, regional levels" leads to "a critical mass of those voices and actions that are necessary for progress and democracy."[63] Likewise, in 2009 she spearheaded the International Colloquium on Women's Empowerment, a conference held in Monrovia that hosted 1,100 women from fifty-four countries, and nine hundred Liberian women, to discuss women's political leadership.[64] She co-convened the colloquium with President Tarja Halonen with whom she composed "The Call for Action," an edict on women's leadership that they presented to the UN General Assembly later that year.[65] Addressing these regional and global audiences, Sirleaf helped promote the link between increasing women's access to governing bodies and practicing democracy in multiple arenas.

Sirleaf modeled how a national leader can put these values into practice within a nation-state. By 2010 Sirleaf touted that Liberia had "six female Cabinet Ministers out of 21," women in 40 percent of local government posts, women superintendents in six out of fifteen counties, and women in 30 percent of junior minister posts.[66] To elect women to office, Sirleaf helped establish the Angie Brooks International Centre for Women's Empowerment, Leadership Development, International Peace, and Security, an outcome of the International Colloquium. The center supports the Gender is My Agenda Campaign, an NGO that monitors and ensures fair elections in Liberia and in Africa.[67] Developing and promoting these resources and practices, Sirleaf not only empowered women as local and national political actors, but in the process she also engaged regional and global audiences, enacting the type of rhetorical leadership necessary to enable cosmopolitan nationalist practices.

Sirleaf's rhetorical efforts also enabled rural and impoverished women to organize and become local leaders. She brought together three UN agencies and the International Fund for Agricultural Development to organize rural women into association, hold elections, and choose community leaders.[68] Like her educational and antirape policies, her leadership initiatives, Sirleaf argued, enabled Liberian women as rhetorical actors and leaders of their communities. To the UN General Assembly in 2012, she said, "We meet with our women rural leaders who are there, they can stand up and say to us, 'We now know what our rights are. We now know what our potential is. We now know what we can do. We can go into a meeting, a town hall meeting that's usually led by men, but we can go there and we can stand up, and we can say what we want. We can tell them that we have a right.'"[69] Mainstreaming women into politics could take hold at the local and national level. Both strategies helped cultivate women into rhetorical leaders and helped normalize the value of women's leadership.

To Sirleaf these measures and initiatives not only enabled women to access political spaces and positions, but they also allowed women to transform what it meant and how to practice politics. She argued that women possessed "special natural skills and sensitivities that many times are lacking in their male counterparts."[70] To an audience of African heads of state and dignitaries, she argued that with the appropriate support, women would lead Africa in development. She said, "Women have historically demonstrated they can be good and strong and bold and innovative leaders. Their commitment to democracy and social justice are often unsurpassed. They are fair, they are inclusive."[71] Invoking the previous groundswell of women's pro-peace activism, Sirleaf redefined democratic leadership as an unrelenting drive to achieve social justice. Likewise, at an international labor conference, she asserted that African women's "strength and determination to influence national decisions was propelled by their blood, sweat, and tears."[72] Women's political leadership, then, fortified the democratic process as an unrelenting pursuit of justice. Quite simply, she said, "transformative leadership is women's leadership."[73]

Including women as policymakers at the national level, then, enabled women to practice and shape politics in Liberia, Africa, and the world. Through a series of metaphors, for example, Sirleaf endowed women with unmitigated momentum and power. She said, as "recipients of the torch that our predecessors passed on," women possessed a "new all-encompassing power" that would bring "a tidal wave of revolutionary change."[74] With this power, she continued, "women nowadays are not only breaking through the glass ceiling, we are shattering it and erecting new structures. We are pushing the envelope and sliding through the boundaries."[75] The metaphors of torches, tidal waves, and shattered glass share tenors of force, movement, and indomitability. The actions of passing, erecting, pushing, and sliding also suggest that women are adept at the give-and-take and push-and-pull dialectics endemic to policymaking. As such, Sirleaf believed that, in practice, women would transform politics *and* engage its existing structures in order to advance policy change for women.

Viewing women as agents of both transformation and transaction allowed Sirleaf to craft a narrative of the inevitability and the effectiveness of women's leadership around the world. Once women's transformative powers secured them in all levels of politics, then they would engage in effective political transactions. To an international audience, Sirleaf said of women, "We are too good not to insert ourselves in the decision making processes that will develop our villages, communities, cities, towns, municipalities, nations, and the entire globe."[76] Women's leadership was key to deepening democracy worldwide. She once said, "Democracy is becoming a global entitlement with women as a critical force."[77]

Ultimately, as Sirleaf promoted the value of women as policymakers, especially Liberian women, and as she enabled women to lead in Liberia, she helped normalize inclusive, fair, and socially just leadership as citizenship practice. As women led Liberia in local government, the national legislature, and as cabinet ministers, they helped transform how to practice politics as well as what kinds of policies were passed—the kinds that sought to empower and include marginalized groups. Doing so helped move women's leadership away from the exception, from necessity in extraordinary circumstances, to the new norm in everyday circumstances. Moreover, as women practiced political leadership within the nation, they fashioned the leading of local, national, regional, and global communities as cosmopolitan citizenship practice, as beneficial to all of humankind.

Marketing and Entrepreneurship as Cosmopolitan Practice

Cosmopolitanism has historically been associated with the elite practices of travel and trade around the world.[78] More recently, however, political and rhetorical theorists posit cosmopolitanism as a theory and practice that seeks to undo the abuses of global capitalism, especially those endured by women.[79] Women in developing nations are disproportionately subject to displacement, trafficking, and poverty, and thus are often forced to live nomadic and migratory lives.[80] In Africa especially, market women and rural women must travel at great cost and risk in order to feed their families and make a living. Ideally, a cosmopolitan perspective of these practices asks how women from within their local, material realities can contribute to local, national, regional, and global communities. However, scholars stop short of asking how this perspective can promote these contributions globally, codified nationally, and in turn transform travel and trade into empowered economic practice. Sirleaf's policy rhetoric demonstrates how these goals can be achieved. First, she promoted the value of women's labor to supranational, regional, and private audiences. Second, with resources from multiple actors, she argued Liberian women could assert themselves as profitable market women and entrepreneurs, ensuring Liberia's livelihood and boosting regional and global economies. Last, she reframed what it meant to participate in Liberia's economic destiny by normalizing market trade and entrepreneurship as cosmopolitan citizenship practice.

Before analyzing Sirleaf's economic policy for women, it's important to understand what women's financial independence meant in Liberia. In Liberia and in most of rural Africa, market women gather and trade agricultural goods. Often these women travel great distances across national borders to trade goods and earn wages to support their families. During Liberia's civil wars, many market women died at the hands of rebels and soldiers or faced heavy penalties for trading on the turf of rival factions. Most market women were illiterate and were exploited by trade partners, ensuring that they remained impoverished. When market women sold their goods in Liberia, they brought their children to their claimed "stall" alongside a road, and sat for hours without shelter.[81] Journalist Helene Cooper describes the condition of a market woman when Sirleaf took office: "[She is] a woman who has literally foraged in the forests for years for food to sell, who has learned that she can depend on nothing more than her own wits and grit and wheelbarrow filled with precious jars of evaporated milk and bags of palm kernels to provide her with the dirty Liberty dollars to feed her family."[82] Cooper argues that market women who sold their wares in Monrovia initially resisted Sirleaf's orders to clear the streets. She said, "Liberia had been a lawless no-woman's-land for two decades; it would take much more . . . to undo years of habit born out of desperation."[83]

Seeking to reverse these conditions, Sirleaf promoted the value and practices of market women to national survival as she assembled money and resources from the UN, national governments, and private interests.

Figure 4   Women and girls work in the Paynesville Market, one of the markets
renovated by the Sirleaf Market Women Fund.

Specifically, she drummed up support and money for the Sirleaf Market Wom-
en's Fund (SMWF), praising and making visible market and rural women's
labor as crucial to national survival. Sirleaf reflected on this rhetorical strategy: "I always make sure to mention the market women in my speeches. In
this way, I am able to bring and keep visibility on an integral segment of our
country that is usually kept invisible in many economies across Africa."[84]
At a fundraiser in New York, for example, she said, "We owe much to these
women. They are our country's backbone. They also hold our future in their
hands because their success is ours to share."[85] Across speeches delivered at a
UN meeting in Tokyo and universities in Liberia and Nigeria, she referred to
market women as "courageous business women,"[86] women "who dominate
our trading sector [and] still work under difficult conditions,"[87] women who
"have grown the food, stored the food, marketed the food, served the food,"
and who "have labored tirelessly to combat food insecurity, malnutrition and
poor health."[88] Sirleaf also made market women visible—literally—as she led
market tours to global leaders, including Presidents Bill Clinton, Michelle
Bachelet, and Tarja Halonen. In national, regional, and global spaces, Sirleaf
promoted market women as key to the nation's livelihood.

While Sirleaf built programs and amassed funds that enabled Liberian market women as ideal economic actors to an extent, she reinscribed the worldist power dynamics that also constrained Liberian women. As many transnational feminist scholars have argued, discourses that idealize "empowered" Third World women as "good" capitalists reify the neoliberal, political economy that positioned them as Third World women in the first place.[89] Consider that her rhetorical efforts successfully raised millions of dollars from the Clinton Foundation, the UN Women's Fund for Gender Equality, the AWDF, and a host of private donors to build and renovate thirteen Liberian markets.[90] Funding the SMWF falls in line with the Clinton Foundation's mission. One of its five central issues is "Girls and Women," aimed at "supporting women farmers and entrepreneurs."[91] Many foundations like this have lent market and rural women microcredit loans, offered them training in sustainable farming, and taught them basic business skills. However impactful these foundations are, critics of globalization's exacerbated effects on Third World women and children point to the political economy that disadvantaged rural women in the first place (let alone the fact that Clinton's presidency was marked by its promotion and facilitation of globalization). Thus, the enabling and constraining dynamics of globalization along with the spread of democracy and capitalism (summed up in the adage "the twin engines of progress and prosperity") cast Sirleaf's discourses about market women as both a symptom and a remedy to the human costs of global capital.

That said, her rhetorical efforts produced measurable effects. One market alone, as Sirleaf announced at an African Union meeting, allowed seven thousand market women to trade goods in a modern facility.[92] In New York she announced that the new markets provided "daycare and primary schools where the kids can go to the school, and we make sure that they have basic sanitation facilities and water."[93] They also provided "literacy training programs," which, as Sirleaf reported to a host of SMWF partners, "has improved their lives exponentially. It has given them the power to reverse the trend of being victims. They can now count their change. They can now write their names. They can now read signs of buildings over their heads."[94] To enable safer travel, one of Sirleaf's programs afforded many market women motorbikes: "We gave each of them a motorbike," she said, "so we have great rural women motorcyclists who go around and carry their message."[95] All of these practices, to Sirleaf, not only empowered market women as "role models for their children, their peers, and others in their communities" but also helped build "a stronger nation."[96] Perhaps Sirleaf's rhetoric worked to assimilate Liberian women into a global culture that values women's bodies for the labor and capital they produce, but it also worked to expand on the impact of women's work to include security for themselves and their families *and* destabilized women's economic output as the measure of good national citizenship. Sirleaf promoted market women as ideal cosmopolitan citizens.

Likewise, Sirleaf's rhetorical efforts helped launch national programs that enabled women as entrepreneurial actors. The World Bank Economic Empowerment of Adolescent Girls and Young Women and the Goldman Sachs 10,000 Women programs, for example, brought together global actors to effect national change. She touted the support of the Clinton Foundation, the Nike Foundation, the Government of Denmark, the World Bank, and private investment companies. As of October 2012, these programs provided entrepreneurial training to 2,491 Liberian women and girls and small business training to 250 Liberian women.[97] Sirleaf promoted these programs in international spaces to world leaders at a women's conference in Spain, a World Bank Seminar in Tokyo, and the Clinton Foundation in New York. Addressing the first class of graduates of the 10,000 Women program, Sirleaf asserted that the program served "girls who need to believe that they can shape their own destiny."[98] Once girls believed in themselves, then they could help rebuild the nation. Sirleaf addressed the graduates as "business people that our country depends upon to lift itself."[99] She praised them as an "investment," declaring, "Investing in women yields the biggest dividends in any country's development."[100] Expanding on economic metaphors, she continued, "Countries that have not mobilized the incredible potential of one half their population—the women—are waking up to this untapped resource. We, in Liberia, know that all the iron ore, gold and diamonds in the ground, or oil off the shores, will never be as valuable as our citizens, with their skills, ideas and dedication."[101] While Sirleaf's economic metaphors reified the commodification of women's labor, they also suggest that Sirleaf valued more than women's earnings: their "skills, ideas, and dedication" could not be measured in dollars in the way that gold, oil, or iron ore could. Their value was immeasurable.

Sirleaf's economic policies and initiatives constructed women's mobility and financial savvy as cosmopolitan citizenship practice. Instead of viewing women's cross-border trading as illegal or a transgression of national loyalty, Sirleaf helped audiences view cross-border trading as heroic, courageous, and foundational to national, regional, and global survival. Sirleaf viewed marketing and entrepreneurship as part of the transnationalization of Africa, wherein the porousness of national boundaries enabled regional transformation. When delivering a Nelson Mandela Annual Lecture to African leaders, for example, she said, "The African Renaissance is being built, every day, by African people—when people reach out, across boundaries—real or imagined. They are not waiting for the Renaissance to be determined by states alone for they know that they are a part of an interconnected world."[102] To Sirleaf Liberians were central to building this interconnected world. At a state dinner in Ghana, for example, she said, "Liberia is committed to seeing strong integration in West Africa where political boundaries will disappear and where our people will develop a true sense of belonging, moving freely and living wherever they choose."[103] The free movement of people—and in this case, of women—not only fortified national belonging but also regional belonging. In contrast to national policies that define citizenship belonging parochially, in a way that restricts citizens' actions and loyalty to "the nation," Sirleaf promoted national policies that defined citizenship belonging as premised on citizens' movement across places and borders. Her policy rhetoric of women's economic empowerment shaped how citizenship was practiced in the new democracy—as women traded skillfully, traveled freely, and ran businesses successfully, they fashioned a cosmopolitan citizen ideal.

Conclusion: Cosmopolitan Rhetorical Leadership, Belonging, and Feminism

In this chapter I have demonstrated how cosmopolitan theory might work in practice, especially through national leadership and policy rhetoric. Specifically, this case study illuminated how a national leader's rhetoric can normalize cosmopolitan values in the global arena, enable practices in a national arena, and transform national citizenship into cosmopolitan citizenship. I've suggested that a national leader use their global and regional influence to address audiences of world leaders and extol the values of education, protection from violence, access to political leadership, and economic empowerment as the means toward a more emancipated humanity. Moreover, a leader can promote the practice of codifying these values at the national level. To enable cosmopolitan practice, this study suggested that new initiatives and policies make it possible for previously excluded groups to participate in local and national communities, particularly in ways that have far-reaching effects on regional and global communities. Moreover, as citizens access these resources and contribute to these communities, national leaders can tout the policy's success to audiences around the world, putting forward a vision of how these newly enfranchised citizens are transformed into rhetorical actors and community leaders.

Transforming national citizenship into cosmopolitan citizenship, as this particular case study demonstrated, fuses the *what* and the *how* of citizenship practice. Indeed, as new citizenship practices (the *what*) were made available, the ways in which citizenship was practiced (the *how*) were altered. Particular acts included speaking out against rape and going to school at least through ninth grade; running for national office, attending and speaking at local meetings with men, and pushing fair and just policies; and selling goods at the marketplace, driving motorbikes across borders, starting a small business, and learning basic mathematics. Ideally, in the process of performing these acts, women enacted a new mode of citizenship, one that pushed back against masculine modes of citizenship, especially since many of these policies and practices targeted women specifically. This new mode of citizenship engagement envisioned these everyday acts as greater than a means to an immediate end (for example, attending school, speaking at a local meeting, counting change). They were viewed as part of broad and deep change, socially, politically, and economically. These acts reflected a commitment to stemming patriarchy and altering gendered beliefs, transforming democracy into an inclusive and just process, and empowering the vulnerable and the poor. As women accessed newly available resources and practices, they fashioned a commitment to empowering themselves, their nation, their region, and the world.

This chapter also exposes how a national leader's cosmopolitan rhetoric can work to include a previously excluded or disenfranchised group. When it comes to the emancipatory functions of a cosmopolitan perspective, most theorists speak broadly. Ulrike M. Vieten's claim is illustrative: cosmopolitanism seeks to "integrate perplexity, multidimensionality, and diversity" into a community's worldview.[104] This chapter addresses how such a perspective can focus on one particular group's exclusion from the national community. Specifically, Sirleaf's cosmopolitan perspective focused on empowering women and girls to participate in the new nation-state as fully enfranchised citizens. Yet a cosmopolitan perspective did more than include a previously excluded group into a national community. A cosmopolitan perspective sought to *include* and *transform*. Women were not only included as citizens with certain inalienable rights but also were granted certain privileges that allowed them to enact a new, ideal mode of citizenship, one that placed themselves at the center of national life, and one that contributed to an empowered humanity beyond their local and national communities. Thus, Sirleaf's cosmopolitan rhetorical practices could serve as a model for how cosmopolitanism includes the previously excluded and transforms national citizenship at the same time.

Viewing cosmopolitanism as citizenship *practice*, it's important to gauge the effectiveness of Sirleaf's rhetorical strategies. As is the case with all policy discourses, they are simultaneously enabling and constraining. Politically speaking, since Sirleaf's inauguration in 2005, representation of women in the House of Representatives has dropped from 12.5 percent to 7 percent; the number of women in the Senate has dropped from five to four (out of fifteen); and currently men lead all political parties, suggesting, perhaps, some backlash to Sirleaf's promotion of women in politics.[105] That said, some of Sirleaf's efforts to mainstream women into government have taken hold. The number of women police officers increased from 6 percent in 2007 to 17 percent in 2016. Studies show that an increase in the number of women police officers improves the rate of reported instances of sexual assault.[106] Approximately 45 percent of those reported rape cases result in arrest. However, many cases go unreported and current studies show that somewhere between 60 and 90 percent of women and girls still experience sexual violence.[107] In terms of Sirleaf's education initiatives, more and more girls attend primary and secondary school, although recent studies show that at least one in five girls experiences sexual harassment by teachers in exchange for passing grades. Some parents encourage their daughters to suffer the abuse in order to stay in school.[108]

That said, in 2013 in the beginning of Sirleaf's second presidential term, the women of the traditional "bush" society for girls, the Sande, insisted on conducting female genital mutilation and on keeping girls out of school.[109] Although Sirleaf's patrilineage stems from the bush societies, she was vehemently against keeping girls out of school. Sirleaf felt so strongly that she went to her family's home county to confront the Zoe, "the name for the traditional head of the Sande Bush."[110] According to Cooper, Sirleaf was "visibly agitated," lectured, and yelled at the Zoe in fluent Americo-Liberian: "'Y'all want the government to make some strong law! We will make strong law! Youn't hearing what I say but next month business, if I come here next month and those girls not in school, you and myself will fight!'"[111] No doubt, Sirleaf was serious about implementing the laws passed to ensure girls attend school through the ninth grade.

At the end of Sirleaf's first term, most agreed that "the majority of Liberians, at every level of society were better off than they had been before" Sirleaf's election.[112] Sirleaf's marketing and entrepreneurial programs provided more women with business skills, although the majority of Liberian women and children still live in poverty. Cooper observes, "Children were still more likely to be found begging in the street than sitting in a classroom" and many market women in Monrovia still refused to move "their stalls from the side of the road to newly constructed markets built to relieve traffic."[113] Interviews with Liberian market women, however, suggest that Sirleaf's rhetoric of economic empowerment has helped women see themselves as agents of change. Linda Howard-Diawara, for example, says, "[Liberian] women can see themselves differently: 'Well, war may have happened, but I've become somebody.' If a woman has money, she's not looking for a man to take care of her. She's able to make sound decisions for herself."[114] Nonetheless, the trauma of war has not faded for many women. Regarding the implementation of a postwar recovery program, one woman said, "We don't want to explain it to anyone again. We don't want the memory to come back. If those people [leaders of the program] come back, I will just close my mouth and cry."[115] While it will take years to gauge the social, political, and economic effectiveness of Sirleaf's cosmopolitan rhetoric and policies, it's clear that the process of undoing the patriarchal mores of a postconflict culture is much more arduous than undoing patriarchal policies.

Finally, because this chapter's case study centers on women's belonging, it advances an inductive argument for a feminist perspective on cosmopolitan rhetoric. If we consider that two-thirds of the 781 million illiterate adults in the world are women, that one-fifth of women are victims of sexual assault, and that seven out of ten of those living in poverty are women, then a cosmopolitan perspective must consider a more empowered humanity as one comprising empowered women and girls.[116] Few theorists of cosmopolitanism have made this connection explicit. Pnina Werbner, for example, argues that a feminist perspective on cosmopolitanism shapes a "cosmopolitan consciousness," one that views cosmopolitanism's broader perspective as a rejection of existing, oppressive norms and an embrace of norms that harmonize the local with the global.[117] As Vieten summarizes, cosmopolitan consciousness "captures the potential power of cosmopolitanism as an everyday habit based on resistance to norms that reflect social closure. In this regard, cosmopolitan consciousness upholds the political potential to change social reality."[118] This particular study demonstrated how the development of a cosmopolitan consciousness could be enabled through rhetorical practice and national policy change. Sirleaf's promotion of cosmopolitan values in the global arena, especially as they work to empower women and girls; her orchestration of policy change and initiatives that made resources available to women and girls; and her promotion of these women and girls as change agents stemmed from a view that cosmopolitanism rejects the acceptance of a reality steeped in patriarchy. Thus, to rhetorical critics and theorists interested in the rhetorical power of national leaders, it's necessary to examine how their rhetoric can foster or limit a cosmopolitan consciousness. Moreover, in light of our field's robust commitment to women's rights and feminist discourses, it's also necessary to study how women leaders craft ideals of women's belonging, in traditional and revolutionary ways. If, as this case study has demonstrated, normalizing, enabling, and transforming certain cosmopolitan values and practices hinge on the will and rhetoric of a national leader, especially one with a deep commitment to women's rights, then it's necessary to craft a feminist cosmopolitan perspective, one that asks after the rhetorics of women leaders specifically for how they seek to empower women globally, regionally, nationally, and locally.

3

BELONGING AS CONNECTIVITY:
MICHELLE BACHELET'S TRANSNATIONAL GOVERNANCE

Sirleaf's rhetoric of cosmopolitanism promoted and helped normalize Liberian women as social, political, and economic actors who shaped their local, national, and global communities. Sirleaf averred that Liberian and West African women would segue from peacemaking to peacebuilding to fortifying democratic practices worldwide. The work of Liberian women during and after the civil wars corroborates the veracity of Sirleaf's claim. For example, as refugees in Ghana, Côte d'Ivoire, and Guinea, Liberian peace women organized to bring humanitarian relief to women left behind in Liberia (*LWP*, 15). Some peace women were fortunate enough to travel to international conferences, where they drew inspiration from peace women from other conflict-ridden nations such as Bosnia, Rwanda, and Uganda (15). Some trained at conflict-resolution workshops in Zimbabwe, Côte d'Ivoire, England, Sweden, and the United States. Liberian peace women also attended the pivotal United Nations World Conference on Women in 1995, where they "publicized their struggles and made important connections with women from other countries" (16).

Participating in countless conferences, consultations, seminars, and workshops, Liberian women developed invaluable relationships with peace-seeking women from their region, their continent, and around the world.[1] At a conference in London, for example, Tonia Wiles, a Liberian peace activist, met a Ugandan woman who urged her, "Do not be afraid. Just keep on talking. . . . Dialogue is a very important process. . . . At some point in time somebody realizes that what you are saying makes sense, and there is a turn-around" (15). These relationships, then, not only validated rhetorical practices such as dialogue, but they also helped generate new ones toward conflict resolution. While attending courses in trauma healing in Virginia, for example, Elizabeth Mulbah and Marian Subah developed a workshop curriculum that the Christian Health Association of Liberia implemented and practiced for many years (15). Moreover, as Liberian activist Deroe Weeks found, interacting with peace women from other areas of the continent and the world forged a shared belonging to a community of women committed to peace. After a consultation in Côte d'Ivoire with Graça Machel, Nelson Mandela's wife, and Samora Machel, widow of Mozambique's first president, Weeks concluded, "When you see these other people, the efforts they make to bring about peace to ensure that we don't do the same things all over the world again, okay, it makes you want to do something yourself" (15). For Liberian peace women, these conferences, consultations, and workshops fomented a sense of belonging to a global community of women committed to peace work.

This sense of inspiration and belonging is quite remarkable considering these conferences can often crystallize geopolitical power struggles between First and Third World women, women from the Global North and Global South, and political elites and grassroots activists. For example, feminist scholars have criticized the work of the UN to promote women's rights through its international conferences on women, beginning in 1975 and made popular by Hillary Clinton's instantiation of the "Women's Rights are Human Rights" maxim in 1995.[2] They claim that the conferences advance a "human rights regime" that privileges liberal, First World feminist ideologies and modes of governance.[3] Anne Sisson Runyan argues that because these conferences are typically sponsored by First World Western governments and are attended by well-funded women, they promote liberal ideals of universal rights as well as a "reductive notion of Third World 'cultural' oppression of women as the target for women's rights enforcement."[4] While these conferences can help forge transnational relationships and feminist policy, they can also reproduce the geopolitical power dynamics that the conferences aim to undo. Put another way, women's national belonging can enable or deter their global belonging.

When situated in an increasingly transnational world and when viewed from a transnational feminist perspective, the discourses of women's world conferences help craft belonging between and among women across geopolitical differences and national belongings. Specifically, I argue that when rhetorical leadership enacts and promotes rhetorical practices that work to stem hierarchical, top-down decision-making, women's world conferences engender belonging to a global community of rhetorical actors. These rhetorical practices call forth the material realities and lived experiences of the women that conference attendees represent, galvanizing attendees to create change not only for the women they represent but also for the women they represent around the world. This shared purpose can collectivize attendees across national belongings into a global community of transnational connectors.

This analysis relies on the interplay between transnational feminist theory and feminist rhetorical criticism, especially in terms of how each field engages the concept of agency. Over the last two decades, feminist rhetoricians have ignited a robust scholarly conversation centered on how globalization has exacerbated oppressive conditions for women and how it has motivated transnational change for women's rights.[5] Throughout, scholars embrace transnational feminism as a critical perspective and form of activism that views national boundaries as powerful and increasingly porous and thus as sites of oppression and negotiation for power.[6] This trajectory of transnational feminist scholarship takes seriously Aiwha Ong's understanding of "trans" as something that "denotes travel through space or across lines, as well as changing the nature of something."[7] Critics are called to account for how rhetorics travel between and among local, global, national, and supranational communities, as well as to unpack how this circulation produces "heterogeneous and interconnected meanings" of particular symbols.[8]

With these tasks in mind, critics have traced how supranational bodies write women's rights policies that "network," "traffic," and "transcode" differently across national contexts;[9] how the rhetorical performances of women heads of state constitute a discourse of "women world leaders" that circulates globally;[10] how the deployment of images via global media can reinforce narratives of Third World women and corroborate with global and national security ideologies;[11] and how refugee policies can serve nationalist projects.[12] Representative of a rich body of scholarship, these studies spotlight the practices that effect "transnational connectivities" or "transnational networks and connections" that enable particular "subjects, technologies, and ethical practices" to circulate transnationally.[13]

As I argued in the introduction, theories of transnational feminism challenge notions of rhetorical agency as located in the speaker and speech text. In studies of transnational feminism, agency is often ascribed to forces and bodies greater than the individual, such as ideologies (i.e., patriarchy, neoliberalism), shared practices and norms (i.e., market trade, cultural rituals, social interactions), and institutions (nation-states, NGOs, the UN). Rebecca S. Richards's work on women world leaders provides one of the few studies that spotlights the rhetorical agency of political elites. Even so, as Rebecca Dingo observed, she explicitly moved away from the "good woman speaking well" model in order to account for how women's rhetorical performances circulated among more global narratives about women's national leadership—placing greater emphasis on discourses *about* leaders than on discourse *of* leaders.[14] Productively, to view agency as contingent and negotiated is to push against "leader-centered rhetorical criticism" and to resist the totalizing practice of ascribing change to the "lone hero" rhetor.[15]

This conception of agency, however, de-emphasizes how, within and amidst multiple agentic forces at play, women assert rhetorical agency as situated and concrete rhetorical practices. That is not to say that transnational feminist theory is unable to attend to concrete assertions of agentic power. Nancy Naples and Manisha Desai, for example, highlight how women can exploit global economic and political structures as a "transnational political stage" to assert agency as local activists, members of community NGOs, and national and transnational networks.[16] Myra Marx Ferree and Aili Mari Tripp especially locate transnational feminist practice at women's world conferences where women can create an "opportunity structure" amidst oppressive forces for positive change.[17] What is missing from rhetorical studies of transnational feminism, in my view, is the critic's ability to account for how women practice this agency and contribute to the circulation of discourses about women's rights. Put another way, if scholars seek to understand the rhetorical dimensions of transnational feminism, then examining the rhetorical strategies at work that can forge transnational connectivities helps to illuminate the complex negotiation of agency at work when attempting to effect global change.

To begin to fill this gap, I take a cue from Ferree and Tripp, who locate transnational feminist practices at women's world conferences. These conferences typically bring together activists, members of NGOs and IGOs, leaders of nation-states, and UN leaders. Because the UN and its conferences have thought to privilege more powerful actors who leverage authority over others to serve nationalist projects, UN leaders have been encouraged to adopt a new model of global governance, one that assumes that nation-states alone cannot effect global change.[18] Situated within the rise of a more integrated model of governance, these conferences facilitate what Ferree and Tripp identify as "transnational dialogues and disagreements" and "transnational mutual learning and sharing."[19] Women's world conferences, therefore, are ideal sites in which to study the rhetorical strategies that negotiate multiple agentic forces to engender connectivities and, in turn, create new resources for women and a more empowered humanity. This wager is grounded in a view of rhetorical agency as a negotiation between a rhetor's choices *and* their discursive contexts, such that inventional strategies are thought to shape and be shaped by transnational flows of political and economic power. This view resists assuming that any single rhetor can effect universal or determined change and instead assumes the contingencies and transience of contexts, political and economic forces, and the shifting sets of rhetorical resources in any given moment. It follows Arabella Lyon's recent study on transnational deliberative practices where she observed, "As participation in cultural and political pro-duction, . . . the work that agency does is not only resisting and sustaining norms, but also navigating norms and the tensions among them."[20]

The goals of this chapter, then, are to offer an example of how trans-national rhetorical studies can examine how women's rhetorical practices engender productive, even if fugacious, connectivities to increase resources for women worldwide. To make this case, this chapter examines Michelle Bachelet's rhetoric as executive director of UN Women for how it created the conditions of possibility for transnational connectivities and enacted and promoted connectivities as rhetorical practice. In 2011 Bachelet was tasked with directing the new UN agency to support state member governments with mainstreaming gender policy and increasing women's leadership in the UN.[21] After four years of negotiating the creation of the agency, the UN offi-cially approved the formation of UN Women in 2010. However, the UN did not grant it the power to create mandatory policy change.[22] Bachelet needed to organize this new agency in a way that collectivized all actors to create concrete change for women despite its limited legislative power.

Following a section that elucidates Bachelet's biography and context, I argue that Bachelet transformed UN Women's annual meetings of the Com-mission on the Status of Women (CSW) into a place where transnational connectivities are made through rhetorical practice. Her specific rhetorical strategies were, first, to make present the women they represent, positioning attendees as an audience that must leverage an immediate response; second, to share her first-person testimony and promote listening as eager recogni-tion of another's pain and witnessing as grounds for political action; third, to position attendees as interlocutors with the women they represent and with whom they must engage in ongoing rhetorical practice in the national and supranational arenas; and last, to constitute attendees as members of a discursive community whose values of inclusion and participation are rehearsed through epideictic occasions that shamed failure and rewarded success. The conclusion argues that this case study encourages a view of rhetorical agency as necessarily inclusive of concrete rhetorical practices at work for transnational feminist change.

Michelle Bachelet's Opportunities and Constraints

The following discussion highlights the situational constraints and opportunities Bachelet confronted as she sought to effect feminist change as executive director of UN Women. Likewise, this section discusses how Bachelet's personal and political experiences helped prepare her to navigate the multiple forces and actors at play in her new leadership role.

The increasingly networked relationship between regional, national, and global actors in the last many decades has necessitated a shift to a new global governance model. "Global governance" is the theory and practice of writing and enforcing shared norms of human rights without a global government. In the past, "global governance" followed "the ideal of negotiating a comprehensive, universal, and legally-binding treaty that prescribes, in a top-down fashion, generally applicable policies."[23] This model worked particularly well in the mid-twentieth century, when nations were considered isomorphic units of power and the sole decision-makers when it came to enforcing treaties and agreements. But in the late twentieth century, when global market forces increased flows of power and goods across national borders and when threats to human life demanded regional and global responses, it became clear that implementing change could no longer rest upon the shoulders of the nation-state alone. A new global governance model seeks to negotiate the tension between the desire for global norms of human rights and the maintenance of state sovereignty. In so doing, such a model must engage multiple actors (IGOs, NGOs, private interests, and national governments) to effect change.[24]

As the nation-state became more entangled with regional and global actors, nonstate groups created what Margaret E. Keck and Kathryn Sikkink termed transnational advocacy networks. Actors of civil society organizations, states, and international organizations form these networks as they build "new links" and "multiple channels of access to the international system," making "international resources available to new actors in domestic political and social struggles."[25] Many of the networks' functions are rhetorical. To Keck and Sikkink, networks "are bound together by shared values, a common discourse, and a dense exchange of information and services" in order to "create new issues and categories and to persuade, pressure, and gain leverage over much more powerful organizations."[26] In short, transnational advocacy networks work to reshape norms and values of national and global governance in ways that will manifest in policy change.[27] For example, smaller NGOs target more influential, regional or international organizations to put pressure on nation-states for greater resources and policy change. Termed "the boomerang pattern," this process is representative of how nonstate actors can create and exploit networks for change at the level of the nation-state.[28]

UN Women's CSW meetings are ideal sites for facilitating the development of these networks and practicing a new model of global governance. The CSW is a two-week conference during which thousands of representatives of IGOs, NGOs, and member states meet, deliberate, and agree on recommended actions for all to take. Initiated in 1947, CSW meetings were led by women leaders of UN member states, while representatives of NGOs attended as observers only. As the UN developed more agencies centered on women's rights, CSW meetings became a place where both UN and NGO actors met and produced recommendations that shaped the UN Declaration of Human Rights and the Convention of the Elimination of All Forms of Discrimination. More popularly, CSW meetings were the sites of the World Conferences on Women, beginning in 1975 in Mexico City, where, for the first time, NGO leaders attended a parallel forum and contributed to the first ever "World Plan for Action."[29] The 1995 meeting in Beijing was where the inclusion of NGOs became "a critical element" to the formation of global policy framework for women.[30]

Upon the creation of UN Women, which assumed responsibility for the CSW meetings and consolidated the power of four UN agencies, the meetings promised to be a more centralized site of transnational feminist change. For example, at CSW meetings, the Inter-Parliamentary Union (an IGO) typically presents data about women in legislative bodies and identifies which nations need more women in those bodies. If, for example, Liberia is identified as a nation in need of more women in their national legislature, then leaders of UN Women would facilitate a meeting between representatives from Liberia and the UN Trust Fund for Women, a private fund that supports women who run for office. These representatives may initiate a strategic plan to identify which Liberian political parties are likely to elect women and which women could run. Further, they may meet with leaders of the Gender Is My Agenda Campaign, an NGO in Africa that facilitates the monitoring of elections to ensure they are fair. At CSW meetings, then, leaders of these IGOs, member states, private partners, and NGOs can more efficiently create new transnational connections and expedite change for women.

Bachelet was no stranger to rhetorical leadership, especially the kind that facilitated rhetorical exchanges among multiple actors. She came off the heels of a presidential term in Chile, which is a multiparty representative democracy only twenty years out from Pinochet's brutal takeover of President Salvador Allende's government. Because Bachelet's father worked under Allende, he was kidnapped and tortured for months until he died of cardiac arrest. Two years later Bachelet and her mother were blindfolded, kidnapped, and taken to detention centers, where they were subject to interrogation, torture, and rape.[31] Eventually, Bachelet was granted exile to Australia.

Throughout her campaign and her presidency, she claimed that because of her life experiences, she understood the needs of the Chilean people, especially women and the poor. Bachelet shared personal anecdotes relating to her struggle to survive imprisonment and torture under the Pinochet dictatorship.[32] She discussed how she tended to the wounds of brutalized women in her cell.[33] These experiences motivated her to become a pediatrician and care for orphaned children while she raised her own in the process. She also shared a story about how, later in her life, she ran into one of her torturers on the street and felt sympathy for the deep guilt he carried.[34] Bachelet's rhetorical leadership practiced the public expression of struggle, sympathy, compassion, and forgiveness. Likewise, she implied that personal experiences of oppression and witnessing the oppression of others are grounds for taking action for the good of the community.

Many argue that Bachelet appealed to the people as a more feminine and motherly figure who would restore the health of the nation and deepen its commitment to an inclusive democracy.[35] Her experience as Chile's minister of health and as the first woman minister of defense positioned her as a strong, national leader. Bachelet's rhetorical leadership has been described as "transformative," leadership that stressed participation, interaction, and consensus.[36] As president she required ministries and public services to create "special commissions," mechanisms by which citizens were included in the "formulation, execution and evaluation" of public policies. Moreover, she pushed for the formation of civil society organizations to work with ministries on policy formation.[37] Scholars and pundits agree that her strategies were politically effective. She led her coalition of parties, Concertación, to reform the constitution, revise the tax code, and expand anticorruption and welfare legislation.[38] As a fierce women's rights advocate she also negotiated with a resistant, male-dominated government to successfully mainstream women's rights into work and health care policies.[39] She is credited with increasing access to Chile's public health system and for making the morning-after pill widely available.[40] Due to a constitutional limit of one presidential term, Bachelet could not run for reelection and left office with an approval rating of 84 percent.[41] Since the fall of the Pinochet dictatorship, Bachelet is regarded as the president who most successfully practiced Chile's "democracy by agreement" political philosophy.

The 2011, 2012, and 2013 CSW meetings were the first three led by UN Women and Bachelet, an internationally recognized champion of women's rights. When Bachelet took the reins of UN Women, UN leaders, member states, IGOs, and NGOs looked to see how CSW meetings might be different than previous ones marked by increased commitments to women's rights but also top-down power dynamics. The following analysis argues that Bachelet's rhetoric helped transform CSW meetings into sites where rhetorical practices promoted the creation of transnational connectivities, which in turn crafted an arena of global belonging for attendees and the women they represent. An analysis of Bachelet's many speeches at and between these three meetings reveals that she made present the demands of the women that CSW attendees represent, shared personal testimony to promote listening and witnessing as ideal rhetorical responses to the women around the world, facilitated ongoing rhetorical engagement with the women that attendees represent in the global and national arenas, and constructed CSW attendees as members of a discursive community whose values of inclusion and participation are rehearsed through epideictic rhetorical occasions.

Michelle Bachelet's Rhetorical Practices

Prior to Bachelet's appointment, various UN leaders ran CSW meetings as part of their administrative duties. Bachelet transformed her role as chair of CSW meetings into that of a rhetorical leader. For example, she opened each meeting with an address to all attendees. Speaking to each meeting's particular theme, she detailed the problems the women of the world faced, outlined the challenges that lie ahead, and charged attendees with finding agreed-on recommendations. In addition to her introductory remarks, Bachelet addressed multiple sessions and side events throughout each two-week conference and closed each meeting with a report of the recommendations and a directive to implement them.

Before moving onto an analysis of Bachelet's CSW rhetoric, it's important to note that her strategies butted up against an immediate scene of bureaucratic and administrative action. Opening and closings sessions of CSWs took place in the UN General Assembly Hall at UN Headquarters in New York. This grand room's focal point is a tall and broad wooden facade that bears the UN logo. Key speakers sit at a green marble table upon a grand stage that faces six sections of twelve rows of attendees. Six more sections of five rows of attendees stretch to the back of the room, where a balcony section seats even more attendees. Those in the back can watch one of the two giant screens that flank the wooden facade. Each section of each row seats six; all seated share a table surface, and each person has a microphone and headphones to listen to a translator. Side events often take place at the Trusteeship Council Chamber, which is not as large as the Hall but is reminiscent of large European parliamentary chambers. Smaller rooms at UN headquarters are similarly well appointed. Altogether, these spaces are not terribly conducive to interaction, conversation, participation, and engaging rhetorical action. They model and reinforce traditional speaker-audience, expert-layperson, active-passive power dynamics that typically work against inclusion and connectivity. That said, speakers typically don't deliver high rhetoric, impassioned speech, or invoke swelling applause. Most speakers read their prepared statements among the ambient noises of clinking water glasses, humming screen projectors, voices in different languages, comments about getting sandwiches and coming back after lunch, and ongoing chatter between attendees. Sometimes representatives from the floor speak from their seats, where they fumble with their translation devices. Even more, sessions and panels typically run ninety minutes or longer, all enveloped by this humdrum atmosphere.

While Bachelet came armed with rhetorical practices and procedural norms that built coalitions and included the voices of marginalized groups, practices that better matched an emerging, networked mode of global governance, her immediate scene constrained her efforts to craft belonging for women around the globe. Not only did the CSWs' setting stymie interactive rhetorical processes between speaker and audience, but it also worked against CSWs as a site of inspiration for change. From within these constraints, Bachelet's rhetoric promoted CSW meetings as sites of transnational connectivities.

Making Present the Demands of the Women around the World

Bachelet's public addresses constructed a rhetorical situation in which the women around the world demanded change from conference attendees.[42] To this end she employed strategies that created presence, or as Chaïm Perelman and L. Olbrechts-Tyteca put it, "the displaying of certain elements on which the speaker wishes to center attention in order that they may occupy the foreground of the hearer's consciousness."[43] They argue that creating presence not only means bringing an image to an audience's mind, but it also means bringing forward certain images or parts of an image to such a degree that they cannot be ignored.[44] This strategy is especially important for rhetors seeking to alert an audience to a particular crisis and to heighten the urgency for change. To that end Bachelet first, ensured that survivors of sexual assault spoke and were heard at the conferences and that their testimonies would directly inform policy. Then, in her own speech addressed to thousands of attendees, Bachelet read aloud the first-person testimonies of survivors of sexual violence. Last, she drew on the surge of women's rights protests around the world, especially in response to violent acts, to situate CSW meetings as an immediate response to those cries. Framing CSW meetings as a direct response to growing protests also flipped the relationship between attendees and the women they represent such that demands for change did not come from within political circles or from political elites; rather, demands came from the women that attendees represent and with whom they must engage.

Bachelet created a rhetorical space for survivors to speak at the conference, heightening a sense of intimacy with survivors and of urgency to which attendees must respond. She asserted, "Policies must be informed by survivors' experiences," and she referenced their testimonies as a "wealth of knowledge."[45] Viewing and counting survivor testimony as legitimate grounds for policymaking reverses the long-held view that personal testimony, especially women's testimony, is unreliable evidence.[46] Over the last many decades, feminist scholars and activists have challenged this assumption such that the experiences of the oppressed count as legitimate sites of knowledge production and evidence.[47] The practice of sharing and counting women's testimonies as knowledge also affirms that survivors, not policymakers nor experts, know best what they need to improve their lives.

For example, Bachelet introduced and addressed rural women at a side event of the 2012 CSW. She said, "Rural women are best placed to determine what their energy needs are and how they can best be addressed. It is for this reason we have assembled you here today; to hear your voices and to understand your priorities."[48] As ideal audience members, then, CSW attendees were to "hear" and "understand" the needs of the women they represent. Video footage and transcripts of that particular forum are unavailable, however, CSWs and other UN Women-related meetings included "survivors' forums" on their agenda. Later that year, for example on December 13, 2012, UN Women organized a survivors' forum as part of a stakeholders' forum for eliminating violence against women. While Bachelet attended the stakeholders' forum, she did not chair the survivors' forum. The chair, Dr. Antonyia Parvanova, a member of the Bulgarian Parliament, framed the forum in similar terms. She asked, "How can policymakers harness the knowledge of survivors and work better with them to prevent and end violence against women?"[49] She then introduced the forum's first panelist, Maria da Penha from Brazil. Via video da Penha shared her experiences as a victim of two murder attempts and as an activist who changed Brazilian laws on domestic violence. Her testimony is quoted at length:

> I am Maria da Penha, victim of domestic violence. . . . I was a victim of domestic violence in 1983 when no women's police station existed to attend to the cases on domestic violence. My victimization occurred in 1983 and the first women's police station in this country opened in 1985. I met my aggressor who became my husband at the University of San Paolo while I was studying for my MA degree. I am a pharmaceutical biochemist. . . . He obtained his naturalization here after which point I could no longer recognize him. He went from being a companion and a friend into a torturer. I didn't know how I could continue in that relationship. I asked for a separation many times but he always refused. And I couldn't confront him. I couldn't face a litigious separation with a man who was highly aggressive even with his own daughters. We lived a life filled with physical and psychological violence. And I could not get out of that relationship. Because at that time I saw myself and what happened. Women were killed when they tried to leave a violent relationship. . . . In general, the aggressor got away without penalty. One day I woke up having been shot in my back. I was in hospital for four months. When I returned from the hospital I was kept in forced confinement for 15 days. During this time, I obtained a judicial authorization to leave my home so I could avoid a charge of abandonment and risk losing the custody of my daughters.[50]

Da Penha continued to detail how her husband attempted to murder her again by tampering an electric shower. He was found guilty of attempted murder twice, but was released due to "legal technicalities."[51] She and her daughters went to live with her parents where she wrote a book detailing her abuses and the injustices of the judicial system. The book wound up in the hands of the international committee of the Organization of American States, an IGO with considerable political power. They censured the Brazilian government for consenting to the impunity of aggressors and for not providing services to prevent domestic violence and take care of its victims. The Organization of American States also recommended a symbolic reparation to da Penha. She said, "That's why the law, 11.340, bears my name, Maria da Penha law."[52] Da Penha speaks in first person, shares painful details of living with an abuser and bearing the brunt of extraordinary physical abuse, and employs a narrative structure instead a deductive one that might recount data, statistics, recommendations, and outcomes. Through narrative, da Penha also exposes the failings of legislative and judicial powers and reveals how her experiences informed and motivated legislative change. Like da Penha, other panelists at the head table recounted their experiences of suffering during violent conflict and how they came to political organization.

While forums such as these held great potential to disrupt the discourses typical of global governance meetings, the women who testified in survivors forums could be said to reinforce "the global progress narrative of victim-survivor-activist" crafted in First World human rights discourses.[53] Moreover, the women were featured in one panel—one panel designated for the stories of survivors. Naming the panel as such highlights its exceptional character; that is, most panels and meetings do not or are not expected to draw on the experiences of the women they aim to serve. However, Bachelet employed multiple strategies to create presence and ensure that survivors of domestic violence and sexual assault testified to their experiences of pain as well as to how their experiences were taken seriously as knowledge to build policy that altered women's material realities. Moreover, these stories often spotlighted the roles of nonprofit organizations to provide resources and pressure nation-states to write and pass laws kind to women. Making present women and their stories, then, can facilitate the generation of rhetorical connectivities between state representatives, the women they represent, and nonprofit leaders.

Bachelet also created the presence of survivors as she read aloud their personal writings. Reading aloud the testimonies of other women, Bachelet functioned as a conduit for their testimonies. Early in her opening statement to all attendees of the 2013 meeting, Bachelet said to her audience in the General Assembly Hall that she wanted to expose "the costs in deep human pain and suffering" through the voices of four women.[54] She read part of a journal entry of an American woman who took her life after being raped: "The pain. The stench. The look of hate in his eyes. Is he still out there? What is left of my soul?" She quoted a young woman from Mali who reported being kidnapped, chained, and gang raped: "There were four of them and they took me to a dark area. Three other girls were also there. They raped us during two nights and each time they came in groups of three, four and sometimes five." She quoted an older woman abused by her husband, who would say to her, "Give me all or I will beat you to death." Last, she

Figure 5   A woman addresses panelists of the Survivors' Forum during the
Stakeholders' Forum for Eliminating Violence Against Women, hosted by UN
Women on December 13, 2012. Photo courtesy of UN Women / Catianne Tijerina.

quoted a young woman from Moldova who was also kidnapped and traf-
ficked: "They were all very drunk and took turns to rape me."[55] Directly quot-
ing these women's voices flipped a script that typically positioned survivors
as powerless victims. Instead, they were positioned as rhetorical actors who
engaged in personal writing practices to record, reflect on, and craft their stories. Recording or testifying to one's own trauma helps reconstruct a reality
for the survivor in which they are the architect. Moreover, Barbara A. Pickering argues, "'Witnessing' enables women to transform themselves from
victim to survivor."[56] The rhetorical process of testifying as a witness to one's
own trauma can enable a process through which women assert themselves
as rhetorical actors.

That said, the fact that Bachelet read these testimonies calls into question
their liberatory potential. The act of recording these testimonies may have
empowered survivors, but when a politically powerful woman reads them
from a global stage in a largely Western, liberal-democratic context, to what
extent does she position survivors as victims and attendees as saviors, saving
"brown women from brown men"?[57] In light of the UN's Westphalian and
worldist historical and ideological underpinnings, these power dynamics are

always at play in discourses of global governance. To another extent, however, Bachelet's rhetoric resists capitulating to these dynamics. She read aloud the testimonies of women of the Global South *and* Euro-American women. Also, she framed these testimonies as illustrations of "deep human pain," calling on her audience to receive these women as humans abused by men, not as victims of geopolitically specific abuses. Further, Bachelet did not read these testimonies for their spectacular detail. She read them for their banality. She followed, "Violence against women and girls remains widespread, and impunity is still the norm rather than the exception."[58] Reading aloud women's testimonies simultaneously invited attendees into private spaces to see and hear individuals' pain and to view these individual cases as generalizable to all representatives' constituencies.

Bachelet also urged attendees to hear shouts and protests from around the world. The night before the official opening of the meeting, Bachelet addressed hundreds of NGO attendees in a UN Headquarters hall and recalled the recent shooting of Malala Yousafzai in Pakistan and the rape of an Indian woman on a bus that led to her death. While the events and locales were disparate, Bachelet described the responses as univocal: "Women, men, and young people took to the streets with signs that ask 'Where is the justice?' with rallying cries that say 'Wake up!'" She expands the global scene: "The momentum is growing and we can hear the rumblings of this call to action among the people, among the thousands of civil society organizations in communities, cities and countries around the world."[59] Through her inclusion of particular, distinct events that provoked similar outcries for justice, Bachelet constructed a global rhetorical situation to which attendees must respond. What's more, she situated NGO representatives as if they could see the signs and hear the rumblings as though they came from outside the conference's doors. She galvanized attendees to respond with the same urgency as those who took to the streets and put their bodies at risk to protest gender-based violence. Bachelet repositioned attendees from organizational representatives to everyday people whose outrage drove change.

Bachelet collectivized CSW attendees—members of NGOs, IGOs, the UN, and member-state governments—as an audience to the women they represent. She created the presence of these women as rhetorical actors with the power to protest for change, testify to their stories of survival, share valuable knowledge, and shape policy. In so doing, Bachelet bound together the multiple actors in attendance—with multiple interests at stake—as transnational connectors who demand immediate action.

The Narration of Listening and Witnessing

Bachelet urged attendees to see themselves within a new global governance model in which they are no longer one another's audience, negotiating for goods and resources within the confines of the conference. Instead, they are an audience to the women they represent, listening to their testimonies and witnessing their pain. Through her narrative of how listening and witnessing personally propelled her into rhetorical action, Bachelet models for attendees what Michal Givoni calls the "care of the witness" by engaging in "the reflexive process of becoming a witness."[60] Shoshana Felman and Dori Laub argue, "For the testimonial process to take place, there needs to be a bonding, the intimate and total presence of an *other*—in the position of one who hears. Testimonies are not monologues, they cannot take place in solitude."[61] In this case, "the one who hears" a woman testify as a witness to her own abuses engages in "reflexive transformations," becoming themselves a witness to another's pain.[62] While delivering a first-person testimony may empower a survivor as a rhetorical actor, it also enables audience members—those who witness and listen—to in turn be transformed into change agents.[63] In other words, Bachelet goads her audiences into a process of self-reflection and compulsory rhetorical action as appropriate responses to the women they represent. Because Bachelet's audience is highly diverse, narrating her personal experiences could ideally maximize audience participation and identification. To Bachelet this moral action, unique to each attendee, stems from and provokes practices including rhetorical listening as eager recognition of another's pain and bearing witness to the oppression of others as grounds for political action.

Bachelet's personal narration worked to normalize the practice of listening as the basis of policy change. Susan Bickford theorized listening as a citizenship practice that takes seriously another's way of speaking. To this end, one must recognize that listening itself takes place within a context of power dynamics. Who gets to speak, what way of speaking, and what gets heard are often determined by "those who control social, political, and economic institutions."[64] As Kate Lacey noted, listening does not presuppose agreement, consensus, or empathy; rather, it's a recognition that, in order to work through conflict, listeners must "attend to" others and their "otherness."[65] Put another way by Krista Ratcliffe, "rhetorical listening may precede conscious identifications," which in turn precedes persuasion.[66] Narrating how she "attend[ed] to others" and their "otherness," Bachelet simultaneously invites attendees to participate in her experience of listening and promotes the practice of rhetorical listening. At a smaller roundtable event at UN Headquarters in November 2012, Bachelet previewed her goals for the 2013 CSW meeting, centered on ending violence against women. She began her remarks with the declaration that behind statistics are stories and asserted, "*I want* these women and girls to be heard in this room today."[67] She then played a brief video montage that interspersed statistics about violence against women and girls between testimonies of Asian, European, African, Middle Eastern, and South American women. One woman described how her husband beat her during her third trimester of pregnancy, another said she was beaten so hard that her hand split open and bled, and another described how her aggressor choked her and told her to take her clothes off before raping her.[68] Bachelet did not spare her audience raw detail.

Bachelet expressed a personal desire to hear first-person testimonies of women's pain, modeling for her audiences an eagerness to understand the needs of women who have suffered. She explained why: "Every time I hear the stories of victims and survivors across the world, I am deeply struck by both the dreadfulness of their experiences and the courage they display in telling their story. . . . Because of the harshness of their daily existence we cannot afford to lose the battle against violence and must go beyond statistics and words."[69] As Bachelet narrates how hearing stories of pain affects her, she models and promotes vulnerability as necessary to understanding the urgency of political work. Through her vulnerability, she encourages conference attendees to remain open to being "deeply struck" by similar stories of pain. Moreover, Bachelet's narration of having the same reaction "every time" infers that she has practiced listening multiple times. Even more, it promotes the practice of eagerly listening to and witnessing others' pain and courage and harsh "daily existence."

In Bachelet's experience, eager recognition of another's pain motivated rhetorical action, especially witnessing. Witnessing functions as a way of seeing and recording an event. Arabella Lyon and Lester Olson argue that witnessing is "a decisive response" to an event so that it can be said to have happened "politically and rhetorically."[70] They continue, "For witnessing and testifying to be a speech act, an act constituting a change by its utterance, the act must be received by a community of action."[71] Through personal narration, Bachelet modeled witnessing as grounds for community action. For example, in a smaller roundtable meeting at the 2011 CSW meeting, Bachelet sat amongst high-level UN leaders and a handful of NGO and civil society representatives to deliver a speech commemorating International Women's Day. She shared, "As a young mother and a pediatrician, I experienced the struggles of balancing family and career and saw how the absence of child-care prevented women from paid employment."[72] Bachelet bore witness to the struggle of other women by sharing this experience with CSW members. Moreover, Bachelet validated the practice of taking community action and policy positions from such experiences. She continued, "After graduating from high school, I decided I wanted to be able to treat people I saw in communities who were suffering from all sorts of preventable diseases."[73] She detailed her journey through medical school and her study of military strategy in Germany and the United States. She concluded, "No wonder I believe that education—quality education, available to everyone—is the most fundamental basis for advancing gender equality and women's empowerment."[74] As a witness to oppression and suffering in her immediate community, Bachelet took action and, in turn, developed a belief that guided policy formation. Thus, Bachelet enacted and promoted the rhetorical practice of bearing witness to the oppression in one's community as grounds for taking action.

Bachelet's narration of the personal enacted the self-reflection and vulnerability necessary for attendees to engage the women they represent and to transform themselves into witnesses. To Govani narrating one's process of becoming a witness has less to do with "produc[ing] empirical or metaphysical truths." "Meta-testimonial discourses" about "the reflexive process of becoming a witness," he argues, has reframed "witnessing and testimony as gestures that are bound to instigate a subjective transformation."[75] Thus, as Bachelet narrated how and why she took to listening and witnessing, she normalized the practice of reflecting on oneself as a witness and, in turn, asking what actions are necessary and ethical to take as a witness. Finally, Bachelet validated these rhetorical practices as generative of beliefs that shape one's politics.

Responding to Demands with Rhetorical Leadership

Because Bachelet promoted listening and witnessing as grounds for taking political action, she positioned CSW attendees as respondents to the women to whom they listened and bore witness. At the opening session of the 2013 CSW meeting, Bachelet declared, "The expectations are very high. I think it is fair to say that the world and its citizens are watching."[76] Throughout multiple speeches at the 2013 meeting, Bachelet inverted her previous strategy, which positioned attendees as an audience to the women they represent, and instead positioned women from around the world as a watchful audience to attendees' responses. She argued that these citizens "look to the United

Nations to devise policies that are strong, multi-pronged and effective."[77] If the world is watching CSW attendees, then they have a moral obligation to act quickly. She asserted that CSW attendees "are vital to women and girls around the world who are counting on us."[78] Swift action, she continued, "is what we owe to millions of women fighting for their rights around the world."[79] If CSW attendees were interlocutors with the women they represent, it was time for CSW attendees to speak and act.

To Bachelet the appropriate response was for CSW attendees to become rhetorical leaders whose rhetorical practices would implement what she called "a new social contract between states and citizens, which prioritizes inclusion, equality, and democratic participation."[80] A few months before the 2013 CSW, Bachelet delivered a speech entitled "The Century of Inclusion and Women's Full Participation" as part of a lecture series in Dublin, Ireland. The speech addressed more than women's inclusion; it espoused her theory of how women's inclusion necessitates a transformation of political theory and practice. She asserted, "We live in a world that is unequal. . . . We need to deal with inequality at the global governance system level to ensure that inequalities are tackled."[81] Through ongoing rhetorical practices, attendees would enact this social contract within the parameters of the meeting and subsequently, within their home countries. The upcoming CSW, then, would function as a training ground for attendees to engage in the rhetorical practices necessary to "tackle" worldwide inequalities. To Bachelet this new contract shifted the onus of political power from one to many. She elaborated, "There was a time when top-down leadership was the mantra. There was a time of belief in the power and authority of the leader. If I am convinced of one thing, it is that to manage today's complex challenges, leaders must first and foremost listen and actively engage all segments of a society, engage people in problem-solving."[82] This shift resonated with the move toward new global governance and transnational advocacy networks that sought to engage all actors in decision-making. This was not a political strategy—a way to gather information at the bottom to inform a decision at the top. Instead, rhetorical leadership was an ongoing rhetorical practice with all necessary actors engaged in dialogue. Bachelet helped normalize the rhetorical practices of dialogue and consultation as the sine qua non of global governance. She said, "Engaging people in development is not a procedural formality, it is our collective duty. . . . People are not beneficiaries, they are partners in development."[83] Reflecting a shift from top-down leadership to inclusive leadership, Bachelet constructed a view of attendees and the women they represent as "partners" or, as I've put it, interlocutors, with whom attendees must engage.

Bachelet's speech in Ireland provided rhetorical context for the upcoming CSW. She advanced the argument that ongoing rhetorical engagement must take place at national and supranational levels. She narrated, "During my life, I have had the privilege to live in service of shared goals for democracy, equality and justice, first for my country of Chile, and now for the women of the world through UN Women. And what I have learned is that leadership is not an attribute. Leadership is a journey."[84] Moving inductively she concluded that leadership is a journey and ongoing, which explained why she would shape CSW meetings and UN Women as sites of ongoing rhetorical practice.

At the 2013 CSW, she enacted the kind of rhetorical practice that promoted leadership as ongoing, incomplete, and grounded in personal experience. In her International Women's Day speech, she said: "I want to use my journey and the collective knowledge and experience all around me to encourage progress towards true gender equality across the world. We will work, in close partnership with men and women, leaders and citizens, civil society, and the private sector and the whole UN system to assist countries to roll out policies, programmes and budgets to achieve this worthy goal."[85] If attendees modeled her rhetorical practices, then they too would shape their experiences as part and parcel to an ongoing, personal journey of national and global leadership. To Bachelet, with experience and knowledge comes engagement with rhetorical actors in communities of action.

Rhetorical leadership within this new contract is premised on many valued practices, listening, inclusion, and engagement chief among them. Others include openness, participation, consultation, collaboration, diversity, and humility.[86] Bachelet put these into practice by structuring UN Women and CSW meetings so that leaders must enact rhetorical leadership. In 2012, for example, she set up the UN Women Global Civil Society Advisory Group "as a platform for regular dialogue between civil society and UN Women."[87] She said, "I have high expectations for this form of engagement with civil society at global and country levels, to serve as an ideas and strategy forum, on key policy, knowledge and advocacy issues."[88] She also called on UN regional offices to set up regional and local advisory groups.[89] By 2013 she reported on having conducted eleven "extensive global public consultations" through "engagement with multiple stakeholders through e-discussions, as well as the synthesis of 176 papers submitted to the consultation."[90] Likewise, thirteen advisory groups had been established at regional, subregional, and national levels, while thirteen more were in the making.[91]

All of these mechanisms—consultation and advisory groups, electronic discussions, and papers—served as points of dialogue and collaboration between

Figure 6   UN Women executive director Michelle Bachelet speaks at a High Level
Parallel Event during the 2012 CSW: "The Worldwide Ban on Female Genital
Mutilation: From the Decision of the African Union to a United Nations General
Assembly Resolution." The event was located across the street from the United
Nations Headquarters at the Church Center for the United Nations, New York
City, on February 27, 2012. Photo courtesy of UN Women / Ryan Brown

and among representatives of member states, NGOs, and the UN. While they
engendered the rhetorical connectivities necessary to effect transnational
feminist change, these mechanisms also allowed Bachelet to promote rhetorical leadership as the means to implement a new social contract. In turn,
she helped normalize rhetorical engagement on local, regional, national, and
global levels as instruments of change. To point, she once said, "I have placed
high priority on personally dialoguing with heads of State, countless ministers,
civil society organizations, and private sector partners to encourage stronger
action."[92] Thus, Bachelet promoted a culture that normalized rhetorical leadership as the facilitation of connectivity among multiple actors.

Crafting a Discursive Community of Transnational Connectivities

Although Bachelet organized UN Women and CSW meetings as sites of rhetorical exchange wherein rhetorical leadership was modeled and facilitated,
the efficacy of those meetings was often constrained by the limited power of

UN Women to mandate or sanction member states. Bachelet organized UN Women and CSW meetings as sites of rhetorical exchange, wherein civil-society actors shared their knowledge and contributed to initiatives and policy recommendations for member states to implement. Indeed, CSW meetings are supposed to conclude after member-state representatives have adopted a list of agreed-on initiatives and policies that will make concrete change for women. So when the 2012 meeting failed to produce a consensus on recommendations, Bachelet was confronted with the reality that UN Women did not have the power to mandate or sanction member states. How then could she ensure a successful outcome in the 2013 meeting? To do so she drew on the epideictic genre's functions to praise or blame.[93] To either of these ends, epideictic oratory rehearses community values to demonstrate how one lived up to them (praise) or transgressed them (blame). This rehearsal of values ultimately functions to shape or share a community.[94] Bachelet assigned blame to the 2012 CSW community for failing to adhere to the values of participation and inclusion. Then, through a "name and praise" strategy, she rewarded committed nations as adherents to rhetorical practice. Together these strategies shaped the forthcoming CSW meetings as meetings of a discursive community that values responsible action and consensus.

In her closing remarks at the 2012 CSW meeting, Bachelet stood behind the green marble table in the General Assembly Hall and defined the outcome as a failure, implying that attendees were to blame. I quote her at length:

> Unfortunately, we have also witnessed an inability to reach consensus on the agreed conclusions on our priority theme, empowering rural women. We have come to an impasse, which is deeply regrettable. The situation is unfortunate and I would like to express disappointment, disappointment that is shared by many women around the world, especially rural women and girls to whom this session was dedicated. It means a failure to adopt agreed conclusions after two weeks full of energy and commitment from so many official delegations, with many headed by ministers and senior government officials. The 2,084 representatives from 435 civil society organizations brought forth the voices and perceptions of women and their contribution was invaluable.[95]

While the outcome was a failure to find consensus, Bachelet implied it was a failure of member states and UN actors to appreciate the rhetorical practices of listening and engaging civil society representatives as interlocutors. Actors not only failed to engage the "voices and perceptions" of the large number of civil society representatives, but they also failed "the women around the world." Bachelet's expression of deep regret and shared disappointment suggested that this failure was a transgression of CSW community values upheld through inclusive rhetorical practices.

Prior to the next annual meeting, Bachelet used the negative outcome as a rhetorical occasion to rehearse the community values of participation and inclusion. On the day before the 2013 meeting began, she addressed civil society groups and acknowledged the "very disappointing" outcome of the previous year's meeting. She assured them, "We at UN Women know the value of civil society's full participation in these, and other important sessions. That is why we contacted the heads of delegations to make sure that they include representatives of civil society."[96] Bachelet reminded her audience that the UN community still valued participation and inclusion of groups who represent women around the world, so much so that they included more NGO representatives that year.

Later that year, when she delivered closing remarks at a UN Stakeholders' Forum, Bachelet incentivized a successful outcome through the epideictic power of a "name and praise" rhetorical strategy. Over the last decade and a half, international affairs scholars have analyzed the media's role in a "name and *shame*" practice, used to publicly shame states and organizations that have violated human rights treaties. Scholars have found that it does not work because it typically results in heightened transgressions and human rights violations.[97] Bachelet employed a similar strategy but with a positive valence: she named and *praised* the governments who adhered to the rhetorical practices of the CSW discursive community. She employed this strategy through what she called the COMMIT initiative to get heads of member states to sign a public agreement to promote women's rights policies in their home nations. At a planning forum, Bachelet asserted that COMMIT urged member states "to announce initiatives to end violence against girls and women and to showcase these commitments to the public."[98] Rhetorically, the commitment functioned on two levels: First, the commitment was for state actors to make public to their nations the prioritization of women's rights. Thus, this was primarily a commitment to a rhetorical act—to "announce" and "showcase" women's rights policies and initiatives. Second, throughout the 2013 meeting, Bachelet employed a "name and praise" strategy to reward actors who committed and to pressure those who had not. More specifically, Bachelet publicly named each member state that signed onto the COMMIT initiative.

In fact, as more signed on, she used her next speech at the meeting as an occasion to repeat the list of those who had already signed on and then to note the new ones. On the second day of the conference, for example, she announced, "Forty-one Governments have committed as of now, and we expect more this week."[99] She then listed each of the forty-one governments. Three days later the list grew to forty-eight governments, the names of which she read aloud.[100] Two days later the list grew to fifty nations, whose names she also read aloud.[101] Instead of explicitly shaming nations who had not signed on, the strategy implicitly shamed nations whose names were not read aloud. Doing so functioned as an implicit shaming of those who failed to engage in the rhetorical practices of showcasing a commitment to women's rights policies. Also, as Bachelet repeated the list and noted the new additions, the strategy created the perception of growing momentum and inevitable change—as more and more governments committed, the perception that change is inevitable grew, and as such, uncommitted governments had better get on board. Thus, the "name and praise" strategy indirectly shamed uncommitted governments for not joining a discursive community that valued inclusion and participation and explicitly rewarded member states for committing to rhetorical action.

Conclusion: Transnational Feminist Change, Rhetorical Practice, and Agency

During her time as Executive Director of UN Women, Bachelet enacted and promoted rhetorical practices as the path to transnational feminist policy and social change. These practices include "seeing" and "hearing" the demands of women around the world, listening as eager recognition of another's pain and witnessing as grounds for rhetorical action, valuing personal experience as productive of knowledge, engaging others as interlocutors in ongoing dialogue, and rehearsing the community values of inclusion and participation. Likewise, she promoted these practices via the enactment of creating presence, sharing personal narrative and testimony, and doling out names and praise.

Bachelet's promotion and enactment of these rhetorical practices spotlights the roles that women leaders play in the formation of transnational connectivities that in turn help effect transnational feminist change. Through enactment, Bachelet spotlighted women's world conferences as sites of rhetorical action, which goaded CSW attendees to engage in rhetorical practices that advance multiple transnational feminist goals, including the constitution of a discursive community; the circulation of ideas, practices, and ideologies; and the transformation of what it means for women to live in an asymmetrical global society.

Returning to the question of agency, this case study helps generalize about the role of concrete rhetorical acts as practiced by leaders, civilians, and community actors in the ebbs and flows of transnational feminist change. These rhetorical acts, such as self-reflection, dialogue, witnessing, listening, testimony, naming, and praising, can constitute transnational connectivities that, as Grewal envisioned, enabled subjects and practices. These subjects can assert rhetorical agency within and between multiple agentic forces, such as global capitalism, patriarchy, and hierarchical modes of global governance. This chapter helps us see how rhetorical acts, expressed by individuals and groups, must be attended to in the scholarly pursuit of understanding what Wendy Hesford called "the production and deployment of symbolic practices and discursive channels of access."[102] While only one of the multiple agentic forces enabled and constrained within a transnational context, the rhetorical agency of individuals and groups can model and promote the "symbolic practices" that materialize, strengthen, and dissolve connectivities that can constitute global belonging.

This study's emphasis on Bachelet as a rhetorical actor risks overestimating the influence of a singular rhetor amidst a dense and complex network of actors, forces, and contexts. Indeed, this study draws attention to a rhetor relatively underexamined in rhetorical studies, which augments efforts in rhetorical studies to "recover, re-read, and re-present Woman in the rhetorical tradition."[103] To that end, this chapter evaluates how Bachelet negotiated her situated context *as a woman* and appealed to her particular audience *of women*, dovetailing works that examine how rhetors produce feminized speaking and writing subjects and strategies that undermine and reinvent masculine subjects and strategies of persuasion.[104] This is very much the case considering Bachelet needed to respond to the exigencies of recent shifts away from top-down, masculine models of global governance and the rise of transnational advocacy networks that can circumvent state power. Moreover, many of the strategies Bachelet modeled and promoted—first-person anecdotes, experience as a source of knowledge, empathetic listening—fall into strategies thought to be particularly empowering for women.[105]

While I am careful to not overestimate Bachelet's rhetorical influence, I think it is necessary to note the limited focus on non-US women rhetors, let alone former presidents, let alone leaders of global governance organizations. All three of these categories warrant further investigation if we want to better understand the potential of rhetoric to shape lives beyond US, male-centered presidential contexts. This is not simply because the subjects that fall into these categories are understudied. This is because, if we adopt a transnational feminist perspective, we must better understand how rhetorical practices enhance and constrain the quality of life for those who suffer in the name of global capital.

Studying Bachelet from a transnational feminist perspective, then, not only sheds light on understudied women rhetors and how they employ and promote empowering rhetorical strategies; it also offers a template for identifying and evaluating concrete rhetorical strategies at work to expand and constrict the quality of life for women, children, and enslaved people. It is necessary to illustrate how Bachelet is one actor of hundreds of thousands working within the webs and networks of civil society groups, NGOs, IGOs, and state governments to mainstream policies toward the education, protection, and empowerment of women and girls. Doing so militates against the idea that Bachelet is a singular, stable self. It enmeshes Bachelet's agency with the social and political forces at play in Chile that facilitated her rise as president and a women's rights advocate, that placed her at the hands of torturers as a young woman, that brought together four UN agencies to create UN Women, that gave rise to neoliberalism and globalization, that proliferated the creation of NGOs and IGOs in the 1990s and 2000s, and so on. Bachelet's speaking moments at CSW conferences are enmeshed but not insignificant acts that can generate, strengthen, and dissolve vectors of transnational connectivities.

Within these networked webs of actors and forces, we can evaluate the empowering potential and limits of Bachelet's rhetorical practices. As I mentioned before, some of her strategies can be considered trademarks of inclusive rhetorical strategies. Creating presence, listening, and witnessing, for example, may work to include and recognize actors typically left out of the deliberation processes at women's world conferences. Naming and praising, on the other hand, may work to exclude state actors who have long participated in women's world conferences. Moreover, Bachelet as the first Executive Director of UN Women may have set a precedent for how subsequent directors lead CSWs such that they include the women represented by attendees and ask them to speak, share, and inform policy design. Bachelet also normalized the input of local advisory groups around the world, creating channels and connectivities for women who do not or cannot attend a conference. Bachelet not only facilitated the participation of women typically excluded, as well as content typically considered taboo (such as the raw details of sexual assault), but she also demanded action from political elites, demonstrating that participation isn't always the result of inclusionary rhetorical practices. In short, when she needed to apply direct pressure to state actors, she did.

More broadly, this case helps us understand how certain rhetorical acts can embolden women who attend world conferences and the women they represent to practice and forge belonging to transnational feminist networks. No doubt, these women are differentially empowered and disempowered, as some are political elites and some are civil-society actors. All, however, are subject to the power and potential of the state. Although the nation-state has become more and more entangled in transnational flows of power, it remains the primary unit through which policies are made and implemented. In fact, many states have responded to the rise of transnational flows of power with virulent state sovereignty. If we are committed to stemming this response, it is necessary to attend to the rhetorical practices that enable belonging to the transnational processes and flows of power that shape national policy.

CONCLUSION:
HOW TO BELONG (OR NOT) TO THE NATION-STATE

Over the past many decades, scholars have examined how women negotiate "global, regional, national[,] and local dimensions of belonging in contexts of both opportunity and constraint."[1] In the main, scholars have emphasized how the global traffic of capital, bodies, and information has constrained women's rhetorical and material opportunities for empowerment, let alone survival. This project emphasizes how national citizenship magnifies and coalesces with these constraining forces, but more profoundly it emphasizes how women created rhetorical and material opportunities through concrete rhetorical practices. Viewed as rhetorical agents who mediate and modulate asymmetrical vectors of national, regional, and global power, women around the world negotiated multiple dimensions of belonging in ways that transcended and redefined belonging as national citizens.

Women forged belonging to places in ways that sidestepped, reimagined, and superseded national citizenship. Situated in a transnational context, these discourses helped us view belonging as denizenship, cosmopolitan nationalism, and transnational connectivity. Women dwelled together and, through shared dwelling practices, transformed belonging from national or factional property to regional leaders of peace. A president promoted and codified the value of women's bodies, leadership, education, and work as the stuff of national, regional, and global democracy. Another woman transformed sites of hierarchical global governance into a global community where political elites and civil-society actors alike listened and responded to one another. Thus, the women under study in this book found a way to belong when national citizenship's exclusionary trappings underwent significant challenges and revision.

This study demonstrates how critics can examine, catalogue, and consider snapshots of rhetorical action as they materialize within an ever-evolving transnational context. To that end these studies employed a method that ascribed rhetorical agency to speaker and to context. They telescoped in and through national and transnational forces to elucidate the conditions of possibility for rhetorical actors to resist and/or accommodate national citizenship. Then each study tracked how rhetorical actors worked within their precarious moments and places to assert rhetorical practices of belonging. Doing so enables critics to track them in other contexts and enables actors to consider them in the process of shifting the oppressive tides of globalization. Moreover, if we layer these contexts and practices atop one another, we can track how these practices network and shape contexts beyond their immediate moments and places.

Rhetorical Acts, Their Moments and Places

One of this book's goals has been to spotlight rhetorical acts as the nodes and the in-betweens of transnational change. Motivated by the rich insights of transnational feminist rhetorical theory, this book has sought a fuller account of how rhetorical acts can punctuate, propel, redirect, or stifle the movement, circulation, and speed of transnational feminist change. Foregrounding rhetorical acts, however, does not mean backgrounding context. Viewing transnational feminist rhetorics and transnational rhetorical contexts as entangled and inseparable, I consider these three accounts of women's rhetorical acts as moments in a broader study of transnational change upon which I lingered a little longer to understand how women have crafted belonging. Thus, this project spotlighted how women have asserted agency as rhetors to transform, network, and move their increasingly networked contexts.

Moreover, this partial and incomplete account of a transnational network of women actors is the result of practicing care toward the women and texts under study. This book elucidates a method of rhetorical criticism that aims to treat its subjects "with care" through rigorous contextualization, a move that tempers the privilege of the critic, acknowledges the impossibility of capturing all vectors of power at work in any given rhetorical situation, attempts to immerse the reader within a precarious and entangled transnational context anyway, and ultimately analyzes the rhetorical practices of women leaders as assertions of rhetorical agency expressive of a moment's conditions of possibility and one's potential to act.

The rhetorical acts under study have included the firsthand testimonies of peace women and, via their testimonies, their acts of dwelling together. These include hosting, sitting with, embracing, traversing, forging networks, insinuating, mediating, lobbying, demanding, shuttling, singing, chanting, and praying. Peace women practiced dwelling in local and particular places to assert belonging as denizens of the homes, roads, conferences, and streets from which they were excluded if not forcibly removed. They also practiced dwelling as denizens of nonlocal places, such as "the land" and of communities that spanned turf, county, and national lines. Drawing on their militant, magical, and ubiquitous power as mothers, literally and symbolically, peace women asserted that they always already dwelled and belonged as a people of the West African region. They illustrated how, in Thomas Rickert's words, "Dwelling is an ongoing never stilled process of attunement, disclosure, and building."[2] In this case, the women dwelled as part of a process of peacebuilding. They leveraged and crafted belonging as denizenship when belonging as citizenship underwent violent transformation. As denizens, peace women asserted culturally situated authority as mothers, reclaimed and repurposed places as homes, asserted belonging to land otherwise violently defended as turf, restored life-giving resources to victims of war, insinuated themselves into political and peacemaking spaces, wielded authority as mediators and arbiters of peace, and transformed public places as sites of militant dwelling.

Ellen Johnson Sirleaf's presidential public addresses modeled the rhetorical acts of a national leader committed to reenvisioning belonging for women. She positioned women as cosmopolitan actors whose social, political, and economic contributions crafted belonging to national, regional, and global communities. Her rhetorical moves include championing transnational feminist values in the global arena and promoting women's rights when addressing international conferences, heads of state, governing bodies around the world, and supranational agencies. Then, to national and international audiences, she promoted the concrete legal and procedural changes she oversaw to ensure that these values were put into practice. By promoting them she not only helped normalize gender mainstreaming at the level of the nation-state, but she also modeled for other national leaders how it can be done. Last, she interpreted for her audiences what it meant for Liberian women to access and engage the state resources Sirleaf's policies helped make available. Sirleaf trumpeted that these women would not just change Liberia but also Africa and the world. These presidential rhetorical acts—promoting, enacting, interpreting—provided Liberian women with resources to alter their material realities, such as schooling, political representation, and adequate marketplaces. These rhetorical acts also enabled Liberian women to make sense of themselves as more than national citizens. Sirleaf's rhetoric encouraged Liberian women to view themselves as cosmopolitan citizens embedded in an interconnected world wherein their social, political, and economic actions fortified democracy worldwide. Thus, when Sirleaf needed to redefine national citizenship, especially to reunite a post-conflict nation, and when previously it was steeped in patriarchy and fierce masculinity, she crafted a cosmopolitan nationalist form of belonging for women. Doing so transformed a violently exclusive brand of belonging into one generative of peacebuilding and democratic practice.

As the first executive director of UN Women, Michelle Bachelet crafted public addresses that promoted and enacted rhetorical practices to curtail the globalist politics of women's world conferences. During her tenure, especially as she presided over CSW conferences, Bachelet positioned attendees as an audience to the women they represent, taking seriously the testimonies of victims shared at conferences, reading aloud the writing of victims of gender-based violence, listening as eager recognition of another's pain, witnessing the suffering of others, using that which was witnessed as a moral impera-tive for political action, participating in a discursive community via ongo-ing consultation and dialogue, and praising public commitments to gender mainstreaming. Ideally, these practices promoted interactions between and among geopolitically diverse women such that they forged transnational con-nectivities, the connective tissues that enable transnational feminist change. During side events, panels, exhibitions, scheduled and impromptu meetings, and conversations, civil society and national and international actors could better engage in sharing resources, information, and contacts toward policy change at the level of the nation state. When national belonging shaped wom-en's world conferences as sites of First World power, Bachelet transformed CSW meetings into sites where women belonged as transnational connec-tors, humanized by listening, witnessing, engaging, and praising the women of the world.

Rhetorical Acts, Across Moments and Cases

While each kind of belonging spotlighted in this study—denizenship, cos-mopolitan nationalism, and transnational connectivity—suited its particular moment and place, each kind emerged as a necessary response to similar constraints. An increasingly globalized and networked world with increas-ingly flexible boundaries of nation-states and national identities threatened to destabilize the sovereignty of national citizenship. Many nation-states that profited from globalization's transnational flows of capital also responded to the threat of increased human mobility by heightening national citizenship's exclusionary power. Throughout the regional, national, and global communities studied in this book, national citizenship entrained virulent masculinity, stifled democratic practice, and structured hierarchical global relations. Thus, when viewed as more than sets of rhetorical practices suited to their particular moments and places, these case studies also expose how these rhetorical practices can create and/or energize a network of national, regional, and global relations. In the spirit of "networking arguments" through policy discourses, the following traces how rhetorical practices of belonging travel across time and place.[3]

These three cases suggest, for example, that when women dwell in response to regional devastation, they shift the local, national, and regional conversations from resolving turf wars to restoring humanity. When peace women dwell on the periphery and inside of peace conferences, they generate recognition and trust as leaders of conflict resolution. They generate support to attend peace conferences and training abroad, where they meet with peace women from their region and around the world. They attended women's world conferences and pushed for the passage of UNSCR 1325, which insists on women's participation in peacemaking and agreements. They position themselves as mothers dwelling with their children, such that a woman is appointed to oversee a nation's first democratic presidential election. That woman's visibility and her success helps promote women as capable national leaders. When civil war rages on, peace women escalate to militant dwelling, such that they protest and pray publicly, normalizing the presence of women in political spaces and politicizing otherwise normal, mundane spaces.

Via dwelling practices, peace women established networks of women between villages and counties that provided the foundation upon which women could campaign for a woman presidential candidate. The campaign came off the heels of a groundswell of women's peace activism, during which women dwelled in public and political spaces, normalizing their participation in political processes and asserting themselves as people who always already belonged to the nation. When some of these peace women attended international and women's world conferences, they likely encountered the presidential candidate's previous work with supranational and regional organizations to substantiate UNSCR 1325 and promote women in peacemaking. The candidate traversed the terrain of the nation, positioned herself as a mother to the nation's men, and identified as a woman who could dwell with women in their war-torn villages and transient homes. When the candidate is elected, she uses her global capital to sing the praises of women's social, political, and economic agency, helping to normalize the values of gender mainstreaming in the global arena. She spearheads national legislation and measures that allow women to more fully develop into social, political, and economic actors. Moreover, these measures ensure that their contributions will transform gender norms, democratic practice, and financial prosperity throughout local, regional, and global communities. The president leverages denizenship into cosmopolitan nationalism.

More and more peace women and civil-society actors have populated local, regional, and international world conferences as more national leaders have normalized and promoted the political agency of such women. These developments have motivated the organization of a unified UN agency for women and a new model of global governance to drive it. The woman appointed to direct this new agency recently finished a very successful term as president of a post-dictatorial nation. She brings with her firsthand experience surviving the unchecked violence of a dictatorship, witnessing the pain and suffering of women and children, and developing a career dedicated to the social welfare of minorities. Moreover, she ensured that the hallmark of her presidency was the inclusion of minorities' voices in policymaking. Bringing these experiences to her leadership of the UN agency, she enacts and promotes rhetorical practices that not only include the voices of the women attendees represent but also collectivize state actors and NGO and IGO representatives as audience members who must bear witness and listen eagerly to their constituencies. After the conference, they must continue the work of dialogue and consultation with civil society and state actors, such as peace women and peace women turned regional and national leaders. Continuing this rhetorical work beyond the parameters of the conference strengthens and generates new transnational connective tissues between supranational, national, and regional actors. These connectivities can enable the circulation, concentration, and diffusion of power, information, and resources necessary for feminist policy change. The denizens, cosmopolitans, and connectors that engage these resources or whose lives are shaped by these policies may enact and promote dwelling practices, democratic leadership, and transnational connectivities that can be brought to bear on civil warfare, postconflict democracy, and global governance.

Rhetorics of Belonging: How to Relate (or Not) to National Citizenship

Together these assertions of rhetorical agency expose how different kinds of belongings can be practiced in tension with national citizenship. Women exercised strategic rhetorical practices in response to the exclusionary forces of national citizenship in ways that not only forged new kinds of belonging but also transformed what national citizenship can mean to women and to violently excluded populations more broadly. Instead of forging belonging that privileged a politics of location (geographic and political locations), the women leaders under study reimagined and practiced belonging that prioritized a politics of relation. Their tenuous statuses as national citizens (if not their denial thereof) provided the shared conditions of possibility in which they related to one another as denizens, cosmopolitans, and connectors.

The women under study in this book helped redefine what it means and how to belong as a national citizen. Women could craft belonging for themselves to a nation and a region as they dwelled together in one another's homes, trekked across dirt roads and turfs to forge relationships and information networks, demanded access to peace conferences, and protested en masse on the perimeters of political spaces. As denizens women redefined national citizenship as inclusive of women in peacemaking and peacebuilding processes. A national leader can redefine national belonging for women as she normalized gender policy in the international arena; crafted policy to enable women as educated rhetors, political leaders, and equipped businesswomen; and reimagined women as members of national, regional, and global communities. As cosmopolitans women could reshape ideal national citizenship as social, political, and economic practices that affected the nation, the region, and the world. A leader in global governance can craft belonging for women as transnational connectors as she reframes women's world conferences as sites where supranational, state, nonprofit, and civil-society actors gather as an audience to the women they represent, to listen to their testimonies and to draw on their experiences as grounds for policymaking; as she models for attendees how to listen to other women, witness their trauma, and narrate one's own experiences of witnessing others' pain; as the leader promotes rhetorical leadership as ongoing dialogue and consultation with civil-society actors and constituents; and as the leader names and praises state actors who commit to rhetorical and political action. As transnational connectors women could assert rhetorical agency as one of many different actors of a larger network of actors engaged in transnational feminist policymaking.

In all three types of belonging, women enacted a politics of relation to one another, as women working together to generate new ways to relate to one another and places. These politics of relation posit belonging as "proper to" communities in tension with belonging as "proper to/property of" places. (Non)belongings as "proper to" or "property of" locations gave rise to belongings as "proper to" communities of rhetorical actors, allowing women to re-relate to places in multiple and more empowering ways. Women could belong to one another based on national *and* regional affiliations, such as dwellers and cosmopolitans of Liberia *and* West Africa. Women could also belong to one another based on affiliations to places that supersede national belonging, such as transnational connectors of a global community.

As part of a broader scholarly conversation centered on exposing the violence of national citizenship and proposing ways of engaging and rejecting that violence, this book has sought to provide answers through studies of rhetorical practice. More pointedly, this book spotlighted the rhetorical practices at work to sidestep and resituate national citizenship. These practices not only generate new kinds of belonging to people and to places but also work to unsettle the tight link between rhetorical practices of belonging and rhetorical practices of national citizenship. While new kinds of belonging emerge in response to and help redefine national citizenship, they also offer avenues to rhetorical practices previously precluded, punished, or mitigated by national citizenship's material and symbolic effects. These practices help dislocate practices and performances of rhetoric from practices and performances of national citizenship. This study of belonging as a politics of relation foregrounds how women imagined new relationships to one another that help create the conditions of possibility to relate to places in new ways. In turn, they can render national citizenship as *one way* of belonging to a community. Moreover, they transformed what it means to belong to a nation-state not only in ways that make room for women and girls to belong but also in ways that position women and girls as the makers, enablers, and doers of belonging.

NOTES

INTRODUCTION

1. African Women and Peace Support Group, *Liberian Women Peacemakers: Fighting for the Right to Be Seen, Heard, and Counted* (Trenton: Africa World Press, 2004), 23–24. Subsequent references to this work, abbreviated *LWP*, will appear parenthetically in the text.

2. Alena Heitlinger, "Émigré Feminism: An Introduction," in *Émigré Feminism: Transnational Perspectives*, ed. Alena Heitlinger (Toronto: University of Toronto Press, 1999); Raka Shome, "Transnational Feminism and Communication Studies," *Communication Review* 9, no. 4 (2006): 255–67; Winnie Woodhull, "Global Feminisms, Transnational Political Economies, Third World Cultural Production," *Journal of International Women's Studies* 4, no. 2 (2003): 76–90.

3. Aimee Carrillo Rowe, "Whose 'America'?: The Politics of Rhetoric and Space in the Formation of U.S. Nationalism," *Radical History Review* 89 (Spring 2004): 115–34.

4. See, for example, Joseph E. Stiglitz, *Globalization and Its Discontents* (New York: W. W. Norton, 2002); Ersel Aydinli and James N. Rosenau, eds., *Globalization, Security, and the Nation State: Paradigms in Transition* (Albany: SUNY Press, 2005); Anthony G. McGrew and Paul G. Lewis, eds., *Global Politics: Globalization and the Nation State* (Cambridge: Polity Press, 1992).

5. Elora Halim Chowdhury, *Transnationalism Reversed: Women Organizing Against Violence in Bangladesh* (Albany: SUNY Press, 2011), 6–7; Rebecca Dingo, *Networking Arguments: Rhetoric, Transnational Feminism, and Public Policy Writing* (Pittsburgh: University of Pittsburgh Press, 2012), 11.

6. "Facts and Figures: Ending Violence Against Women," UN Women, accessed January 17, 2017, http://www.unwomen.org/en/what-we-do/ending-violence-against-women/facts-and-figures/; "Know Your World: Facts About Hunger and Poverty," The Hunger Project, http://www.thp.org/knowledge-center/know-your-world-facts-about-hunger-poverty/; "Facts and Figures," UN Women, http://www.unwomen.org/en/news/in-focus/commission-on-the-status-of-women-2012/facts-and-figures/.

7. Lourdes Beneria, Günseli Berik, and Maria Floro, *Gender, Development, and Globalization: Economics As If All People Mattered* (New York: Routledge, 2003); Jackie Smith, Charles Chatfield, and Ron Pagnucco, eds., *Transnational Social Movements and Global Politics: Solidarity Beyond the State* (Syracuse: Syracuse University Press, 1997); Sanjeev Khagram, James V. Riker, and Kathryn Sikkink, eds., *Restructuring World Politics: Transnational Social Movements, Networks, and Norms* (Minneapolis: University of Minnesota Press, 2002).

8. My use of "community" draws on Robert DeChaine's polyvalent understanding of the term, as the result of ongoing "rhetorical struggles," as something that "evokes feelings of belonging, unity, presence, and wholeness," as well as "an object of hegemonic struggle" that often elicits violent efforts to determine "what a community is and can be." Robert DeChaine, afterword to *The Rhetorics of U.S. Immigration: Identity, Community, Otherness*, ed. E. Johanna Hartelius (University Park: Pennsylvania State University Press, 2015), 277.

9. Aiwha Ong, *Flexible Citizenship: The Cultural Logics of Transnationality* (Durham: Duke University Press, 1999); Ingo Pies and Peter Koslowski, eds., *Corporate Citizenship and New Governance: The Political Role of Corporations* (London: Springer Press, 2011); Luis Cabrera, *The Practice of Global Citizenship* (Cambridge: Cambridge University Press, 2010); Hans Schattle, *The Practices of Global Citizenship* (Lanham: Rowman and Littlefield, 2008); Kimberly Hutchings and Roland Dannreuther, eds., *Cosmopolitan Citizenship* (New York: Macmillan Press, 1999).

10. Robert DeChaine, *Global Humanitarianism: NGOs and the Crafting of Community* (Lanham: Lexington Books, 2005), 10. Emphasis mine.

11. Most often, these citizenship ideals are attributed to Aristotle's vision of the polis in his *Politics*. See Aristotle, *The Politics*, ed. E. H. Warmington (Cambridge: Harvard University Press, 1972). See also Richard Kraut, *Aristotle: Political Philosophy* (Oxford: Oxford University Press, 2002).

12. Benedict Anderson, *Imagined Communities: Reflections on the Origin and Spread of Nationalism* (London: Verso, 2006).

13. From this vast body of literature, recent works include Jason Edward Black, *American Indians and the Rhetoric of Removal and Allotment* (Jackson: University of Mississippi Press, 2015); Karma Chávez, *Queer Migration Politics: Activist Rhetoric and Coalitional Possibilities* (Urbana: University of Illinois Press, 2013); Jay P. Childers, *The Evolving Citizen: American Youth and the Changing Norms of Democratic Engagement* (University Park: Pennsylvania State University Press, 2012); David Josue Cisneros, *The Border Crossed Us: Rhetorics of Borders, Citizenship, and Latin/o Identity* (Tuscaloosa: University of Alabama Press, 2013).

14. A few representative studies include James Aunt Arne and Enríque D. Rigsby, eds., *Civil Rights Rhetoric and the American Presidency* (College Station: Texas A&M University Press, 2005); Vanessa B. Beasley, *You, The People: American National Identity in Presidential Rhetoric* (College Station: Texas A&M University Press, 2004); Garth E. Pauley, *LBJ's American Promise: The 1965 Voting Rights Address* (College Station: Texas A&M University Press, 2007); Isaac West, *Transforming Citizenships: Transgender Articulations of the Law* (New York: New York University Press, 2014); Kirt H. Wilson, *The Reconstruction Desegregation Debate: The Politics of Equality and the Rhetoric of Place, 1870–1875* (East Lansing: Michigan State University Press, 2002).

15. Representative studies include Kevin Michael DeLuca, *Image Politics: The New Rhetoric of Environmental Activism* (New York: Routledge, 1999); Michelle Hall Kells, *Héctor P. Garcia: Everyday Rhetoric and Mexican American Civil Rights* (Carbondale: Southern Illinois University Press, 2006); Darrel Wanzer-Serrano, *The New York Young Lords and the Struggle for Liberation* (Philadelphia: Temple University Press, 2015); Susan Zaeske, *Signatures of Citizenship: Petitioning, Antislavery, and Women's Political Identity* (Chapel Hill: University of North Carolina Press, 2003).

16. See, for example, Amy L. Brandzel, *Against Citizenship: The Violence of the Normative* (Urbana: University of Illinois Press, 2016); Hector Amaya, *Citizenship Excess: Latino/as, Media, and the Nation* (New York: New York University Press, 2013).

17. Cheryl Jorgensen-Earp, *"The Transfiguring Sword": The Just War of the Women's Social and Political Union* (Tuscaloosa: University of Alabama Press, 1997); Belinda A. Stillion Southard, *Militant Citizenship: The Rhetorical Strategies of the National Woman's Party, 1913–1920* (College Station: Texas A&M University Press, 2011).

18. Kenneth Burke, *The Philosophy of Literary Form: Studies in Symbolic Action* (Berkeley: University of California Press, 1973), 61, 293.

19. Aristotle, *The "Art" of Rhetoric*, trans. John Henry Freese (Cambridge: Harvard University Press, 1975). Scholars typically attribute Isocrates's conceptualization of rhetoric to his works "Antidosis" and "Panegyricus," both of which can be found in Isocrates, *Isocrates Volume I*, ed. George Norlin (New York: G. P. Putnam's Sons, 1928).

20. Kenneth Burke, *A Rhetoric of Motives* (Berkeley: University of California Press, 1969), 21.

21. See Celeste Michelle Condit, "Post-Burke: Transcending the Sub-Stance of Dramatism," *Quarterly Journal of Speech* 78, no. 3 (1992): 349–55; Sonja K. Foss and Cindy L. Griffin, "A Feminist Perspective on Rhetorical Theory: Toward a Clarification of Boundaries," *Western Journal of Communication* 56, no. 4 (1992): 330–49. Recently, Debra Hawhee articulated how Burke's theories may align with feminist rhetorical theory. Debra Hawhee, *Moving Bodies: Kenneth Burke at the Edges of Language* (Columbia: University of South Carolina Press, 1993).

22. Karlyn Kohrs Campbell, *Man Cannot Speak for Her*, vol. 1, *A Critical Study of Early Feminist Rhetoric* (New York: Praeger, 1989); Karlyn Kohrs Campbell, *Man Cannot Speak for Her*, vol. 2, *Key Texts of the Early Feminists* (New York: Praeger, 1989); Cheryl Glenn, *Rhetoric Retold: Regendering the Tradition from Antiquity through the Renaissance* (Carbondale: Southern Illinois University Press, 1997); Shirley Wilson Logan, *With Pen and Voice: A Critical Anthology of Nineteenth-Century African-American Women* (Carbondale: Southern Illinois University Press, 1995); Shirley Wilson Logan, *"We Are Coming": The Persuasive Discourse of Nineteenth-Century Black Women* (Carbondale: Southern Illinois University Press, 1999).

23. Key works include Patricia Hill Collins, *Black Feminist Thought: Knowledge, Consciousness, and the Politics of Empowerment*, 2nd ed. (New York: Routledge, 2000); Donna Haraway, *Simians, Cyborgs, and Women: The Reinvention of Nature* (New York: Routledge, 1991); Sandra Harding, *Whose Science? Whose Knowledge?: Thinking from Women's Lives* (Ithaca: Cornell University Press, 1991).

24. See Judith Butler, *Bodies That Matter: On the Discursive Limits of "Sex"* (New York: Routledge, 1993); Butler, *Gender Trouble: Feminism and the Subversion of Identity* (New York: Routledge, 1990).

25. Dow terms these studies as part of the "Recovery Project" phase of feminist rhetorical scholarship. Bonnie J. Dow, "Feminism and Public Address Research: Television News and the Constitution of Women's Liberation," in *The Handbook of Rhetoric and Public Address*, ed. Shawn J. Parry-Giles and J. Michael Hogan (Malden, Mass.: Wiley-Blackwell, 2010), see especially pages 346–50.

26. Ibid., 350–52.

27. Karlyn Kohrs Campbell, "Agency: Promiscuous and Protean," *Communication and Critical/Cultural Studies* 2, no. 1 (2005): 3.

28. Ibid., 5.

29. Michael Calvin McGee, "In Search of 'The People': A Rhetorical Alternative," *Quarterly Journal of Speech* 61, no. 3 (1975): 235–49.

30. Key works by these authors that speak to their positions on text include: Michael Calvin McGee, "Text, Context, and the Fragmentation of Culture," *Western Journal of Speech Communication* 54, no. 3 (1990): 274–89; Michael Leff, "Things Made by Words: Reflections on Textual Criticism," *Quarterly Journal of Speech* 78, no. 2 (1990): 223–31.

31. John Angus Campbell, "Between the Fragment and the Icon: Prospect for a Rhetorical House of the Middle Way," *Western Journal of Speech Communication* 54, no. 3 (1990): 366.

32. Michael Lane Bruner, "Global Governance and the Critical Public," *Rhetoric and Public Affairs* 6, no. 4 (2003): 687–708.

33. Rebecca Dingo and J. Blake Scott, eds., *The Megarhetorics of Global Development* (Pittsburgh: University of Pittsburgh Press, 2012).

34. Dingo and Scott's edited collection of essays in *Megarhetorics* features a section of essays on how groups have attempted to resist megarhetorics but do so with limited success.

35. Dingo, *Networking Arguments*, 8; Inderpal Grewal and Caren Kaplan, "Introduction: Transnational Feminist Practices and Questions of Postmodernity," in *Scattered Hegemonies: Postmodernity and Transnational Feminist Practices*, ed. Inderpal Grewal and Caren Kaplan (Minneapolis: University of Minnesota Press, 1994), 17; Richa Nagar and Amanda Lock Swarr, "Introduction: Theorizing Transnational Feminist Praxis," in *Critical Transnational Feminist Praxis*, ed. Amanda Lock Swarr and Richa Nagar (Albany: SUNY Press, 2010), 3–4.

36. Ong, *Flexible Citizenship*, 4; Woodhull, "Global Feminisms."

37. Marcia Texler Segal and Esther Ngan-ling Chow, "Analyzing Gender, Intersectionality, and Inequality in Global, Transnational, and Local Contexts," in *Analyzing Gender, Intersectionality, and Multiple Inequalities: Global, Transnational, and Local Contexts*, ed. Esther Ngan-Ling Chow, Marcia Texler Segal, and Lin Tan (Bingley, UK: Emerald, 2011), 8. See also Chowdhury, *Transnationalism Reversed*, 6–7; Dingo, *Networking Arguments*, 11.

38. Inderpal Grewal, *Transnational America: Feminisms, Diasporas, Neoliberalisms* (Durham: Duke University Press, 2005), 3.

39. Myra Marx Ferree, "Globalization and Feminism: Opportunities and Obstacles for Activism in the Global Arena," in *Global Feminism: Transnational Women's Activism, Organizing, and Human Rights*, ed. Myra Marx Ferree and Aili Mari Tripp (New York: New York University Press, 2006), 4.

40. Peggy Levitt, "Constructing Gender Across Borders: A Transnational Approach," in *Analyzing Gender, Intersectionality, and Multiple Inequalities: Global, Transnational, and Local Contexts*, ed. Esther Ngan-ling Chow, Marcia Texler Segal, and Lin Tan (Bingley, UK: Emerald, 2011), 167.

41. Segal and Chow, "Analyzing Gender," 8.

42. Dingo, *Networking Arguments*.

43. Rebecca S. Richards, *Transnational Feminist Rhetorics and Gendered Leadership in Global Politics: From Daughters of Destiny to Iron Ladies* (Lanham: Lexington Books, 2015).

44. Rebecca Dingo, "Foreword," in Richards, *Transnational Feminist Rhetorics*, ix.

45. Jacqueline Jones Royster and Gesa E. Kirsch, *Feminist Rhetorical Practices: New Horizons for Rhetoric, Composition, and Literacy Studies* (Carbondale: Southern Illinois Press, 2012), 130.

46. Wendy S. Hesford, "Global Turns and Cautions in Rhetoric and Composition Studies," *Publications of the Modern Language Association of America* 121, no. 3 (2006): 794.

47. Arabella Lyon, *Deliberative Acts: Democracy, Rhetoric, and Rights* (University Park: Pennsylvania State University Press, 2013), 69.

48. Ibid., 76.

49. LuMing Mao, "The Rhetoric of Responsibility: Practicing the Art of Recontextualization," *Rhetoric Review* 30, no. 2 (2011): 119–20.

50. Lyon, *Deliberative Acts*, 54.

51. Ibid., 58.

52. Robert Asen, "A Discourse Theory of Citizenship," *Quarterly Journal of Speech* 90, no. 2 (2004): 189–211.

53. Danielle Allen, *Talking to Strangers: Anxieties of Citizenship since Brown v. Board of Education* (Chicago: University of Chicago Press, 2004), 12.

54. Richard Marback, *Managing Vulnerability: South Africa's Struggle for Democratic Rhetoric* (Columbia: University of South Carolina Press, 2012).

55. Dingo, *Networking Arguments*, 8; Grewal and Kaplan, "Transnational Feminist Practices," 17; Nagar and Swarr, "Theorizing Transnational Feminist Praxis," 3–4.

56. Aimee Carrillo Rowe, "Be Longing: Toward a Feminist Politics of Relation," *National Women's Studies Association Journal* 17, no. 2 (2005): 16.

57. Ibid., 18.

58. Ibid., 37.

59. Karma R. Chávez, "Border (In)Securities: Normative and Differential Belonging in LGBTQ and Immigrant Rights Discourses," *Communication and Critical/Cultural Studies* 7, no. 2 (2010): 149.

60. Rowe, "Be Longing," 17.

61. Thomas Rickert, *Ambient Rhetoric: The Attunements of Rhetorical Being* (Pittsburgh: University of Pittsburgh Press, 2013), 15.

62. Ibid.

63. Thomas Hammar, *Democracy and the Nation State: Aliens, Denizens, and Citizens in a World of International Migration* (Aldershot: Avesbury, 1990); C. Shearing and J. Wood, "Nodal Governance, Democracy, and the New 'Denizens,'" *Journal of Law and Society* 30, no. 3 (2003): 400–19; Neil Walker, "Denizenship and Deterritorialization in the EU," in *A Right to Inclusion and Exclusion?: Normative Fault Lines of the EU's Area of Freedom, Security and Justice*, ed. Hans Lindahl (Oxford: Hart, 2009).

64. James Rosbrook-Thompson, "'I'm Local and Foreign': Belonging, the City, and the Case for Denizenship," *Urban Studies* 52, no. 9 (2015): 1615–30; Duncan Scott, "Negotiated Denizenship: Foreign Nationals' Tactics of Belonging in a Cape Town Township," *Social Dynamics: A Journal of the Centre for African Studies University of Cape Town* 39, no. 3 (2013): 520–35.

65. Most of these transcripts are published in *LWP*.

66. The phrase "dwelling place" is drawn from Michael J. Hyde's, *The Ethos of Rhetoric* (Columbia: University of South Carolina Press, 2004).

67. All of Sirleaf's speech texts are available on Liberia's official website for the president, Executive Mansion, http://www.emansion.gov.lr/2content_list_sub.php?main=24&related=24&pg=mp/.

68. All of Bachelet's speeches are available at "Older Sessions," UN Women, accessed September 1, 2105, http://www.unwomen.org/en/csw/previous-sessions/older-sessions/.

CHAPTER I

1. Doris H. Railey, "Some Impacts of the Liberian Civil War: A Pilot Study of Thirty Liberian Immigrant Families in the United States," *Liberian Studies Journal* 22, no. 2 (1997): 261, as quoted in *LWP*, 8.

2. For a recent treatment of how Liberian women leveraged their maternal authority during the civil wars, see Allison Prasch, "Maternal Bodies in Militant Protest: Leymah Gbowee and the Rhetorical Agency of African Motherhood," *Women's Studies in Communication* 38, no. 2 (2015): 187–205.

3. Jennifer Ngair Heuer, *The Family and the Nation: Gender and Citizenship in Revolutionary France, 1789–1830* (Ithaca: Cornell University Press, 2005); George Lakoff, *Communicating Our American Values and Vision* (New York: Farrar, Strauss and Giroux, 2006); George Lakoff, *Moral Politics: How Liberals and Conservatives Think* (Chicago: University of Chicago Press, 1996); Andreas Musolff, *Political Metaphor Analysis: Discourse and Scenarios* (London: Bloomsbury, 2016).

4. Sumathi Ramaswamy, *The Goddess and the Nation: Mapping Mother India* (Durham: Duke University Press, 2010); Sita Ranchod-Nilsson and Mary Ann Tréreault, eds., *Women, States, and Nationalism: At Home in the Nation?* (London: Routledge, 2000); Kirsten Stirling, *Bella Caledonia: Woman, Nation, Text* (New York: Rodopi, 2008).

5. Miriam Cooke, *Women and the War Story* (Berkeley: University of California Press, 1996), 105–7; Dana Cooper and Claire Phelan, eds., *Motherhood and War: International Perspectives* (New York: Palgrave Macmillan, 2014).

6. Oyeronke Oyewumi, "Abiyamo: Theorizing African Motherhood," *Jenda: A Journal of Culture and African Women Studies* 4, no. 1 (2003): 4.

7. Oyeronke Oyewumi, "Family Bonds/Conceptual Binds: African Notes on Feminist Epistemologies," *Signs* 25, no. 4 (2000): 1096.

8. Olayinka Akanle, *Kinship Networks and International Migration in Nigeria* (Newcastle upon Tyne: Cambridge Scholars, 2013); John A. Arthur, *African Women Immigrants in the United States: Crossing Transnational Borders* (New York: Palgrave Macmillan, 2009).

9. Peter P. Ekeh, "Kinship and State in African and African American Histories," in *The African Diaspora: African Origins and New World Identities*, ed. Isidore Okpewho, Carole Boyce Davies, and Ali Al'Amin Mazrui (Bloomington: Indiana University Press, 1999), 103.

10. These organizations focused on providing food, shelter, medical care, and other basic needs to victims, mediating conflict between neighbors and members of the same village, counseling victims of sexual assault, providing legal counsel, funding women's travel to conferences and to do peace work, leading mediations between warlords, and organizing protests. Throughout Liberia's two civil wars, these organizations emerged, worked, morphed into new organizations, or disbanded. Because these women worked with very few resources—some worked with different regional UN agencies—records of their activities weren't consistently recorded, if at all. If they had a web site, such as the Mano River Union Women's Peace Network (www.marwopnet.org), very few details of their activities were recorded in real time and have not been updated for years. Additionally, I consulted multiple nontraditional, nonscholarly sources that recount women's work during the civil wars. Very few of these sources provide firsthand accounts of their work, and many cite *Liberian Women Peacemakers*, the central source of my texts. See Anne Theobald, *The Role of Women in Making and Building Peace in Liberia: Gender Sensitivity versus Masculinity* (Stuttgart, Germany: ibidem-Verlag, 2013), 50n79, 51n82.

11. J. Gus Liebenow, *Liberia: The Quest for Democracy* (Bloomington: Indiana University Press, 1987), 186.

12. Danny Hoffman, *The War Machine: Young Men and Violence in Sierra Leone and Liberia* (Durham: Duke University Press, 2011), xii.

13. Lansana Gberie, *A Dirty War in West Africa: The RUF and the Destruction of Sierra Leone* (Bloomington: Indiana University Press, 2005), 55–56.

14. Adekeye Adebajo, *Building Peace in West Africa: Liberia, Sierra Leone, and Guinea-Bissau* (Boulder: Lynne Rienner, 2002), 68–70.

15. Ibid., 69.

16. David Harris, *Civil War and Democracy in West Africa: Conflict Resolution, Elections, and Justice in Sierra Leone and Liberia* (London: I. B. Tauris, 2011), 131.

17. Ibid., 131–34.

18. Myriam Denov, *Child Soldiers: Sierra Leone's Revolutionary Front* (New York: Cambridge University Press, 2010), 50; "How to Fight, How to Kill: Child Soldiers in Liberia," *Human Rights Watch* 16, no. 2 (A) (2004): 1. Retrieved from http://www.hrw.org/en/reports/2004/02/02/how-fight-how-kill/.

19. Megan H. MacKenzie, *Female Soldiers in Sierra Leone: Sex, Security, and Post-Conflict Development* (New York: New York University Press, 2012), 41; Yaroslav Trofimov, "In Liberia's War, Woman Commanded Fear and Followers," *Wall Street Journal—Eastern Edition*, August 22, 2003, A1–A2.

20. Estimates are difficult to come by, nonetheless, the World Health Organization reported that about three-quarters of women and girls in Liberia were assaulted, and Human Rights Watch reported that about 275,000 women and girls in Sierra Leone were assaulted. Marie-Claire O. Omanyondo, *Sexual and Gender-Based Violence*

and Health Facility Needs Assessment: Liberia (Geneva: World Health Organization, 2005), 26. Retrieved from http://www.who.int/hac/crises/lbr/Liberia_RESULTS_AND_DISCUSSION13.pdf. "'We'll Kill You if You Cry': Sexual Violence in the Sierra Leone Conflict," *Human Rights Watch* 15, no. 1 (A) (2003). Retrieved from https://www.hrw.org/report/2003/01/16/well-kill-you-if-you-cry/sexual-violence-sierra-leone-conflict/. Toga Gayewea McIntosh, *National Human Development Report: Liberia 2006* (Monrovia, Liberia: United Nations Development Programme), 42. Retrieved from http://hdr.undp.org/en/reports/national/africa/liberia/LIBERIA_2006_en.pdf.

21. Benhabib, *Another Cosmopolitanism.*

22. Neil Walker, "Denizenship and Deterritorialization," 261.

23. Most scholarship on denizenship references Tomas Hammar's definition of denizens: legal, permanent "alien" residents "who are not regular and plain foreign citizens anymore, but also not naturalized citizens of the receiving country." Hammar, *Democracy and the Nation State*, 13.

24. Ece Ozlem Atikcan, "Citizenship or Denizenship: The Treatment of Third Country Nationals in the European Union," SEI Working Paper 85 (Brighton: Sussex European Institute, 2006): 1–49; Rachel Ida Buff, "Denizenship as Transnational Practice: Im/migration, Citizenship, and Empire in and around the Post-1945 U.S.," in *The Transformation of Public Culture: Assessing the Politics of Diversity, Democracy, and Community in the United States, 1890 to the Present*, ed. Marguerite Shaffer (Philadelphia: University of Pennsylvania Press, 2008), 263–72; Ayako Komine, "When Migrants Become Denizens: Understanding Japan as a Reactive Immigration Country," *Contemporary Japan* 26, no. 2 (2014): 197–222.

25. Rosbrook-Thompson, "'I'm Local and Foreign,'" 1615–30; Scott, "Negotiated Denizenship," 520–35.

26. Rosbrook-Thompson, "'I'm Local and Foreign,'" 1624.

27. Ibid., 1623.

28. Devika Chawla and Stacy Holman Jones, introduction to *Stories of Home: Place, Identity, Exile*, ed. Devika Chawla and Stacy Holman Jones (Lanham: Lexington Books, 2015), xii.

29. Martin Heidegger, "Building Dwelling Thinking," in *Philosophy and the City: Classic to Contemporary Writings*, ed. Sharon M. Meagher (New York: State University of New York Press, 2008), 121.

30. Chawla and Jones, introduction to *Stories of Home*, xii; Daniel López and Tomás Sánchez-Criado, "Dwelling the Telecare Home Place, Location, and Habitability," *Space and Culture* 12, no. 3 (2009): 349.

31. Ruth Behar, foreword to *Women on the Verge of Home*, ed. Bilinda Straight (Albany: State University Press of New York, 2005), ix–xi; Homi K. Bhabha, *The Location of Culture* (London: Routledge, 1994).

32. K. H. Adler, "Gendering Histories of Homes and Homecomings," *Gender and History* 21, no. 3 (2009): 455–64; Biddy Martin and Chandra T. Mohanty, "Feminist Politics: What's Home Got to Do with It?," in *Feminist Studies, Critical Studies*, ed. Teresa de Lauretis (Bloomington: Indiana University Press, 1986), 191–212; Julia Wardhaugh, "The Unaccommodated Woman: Home, Homelessness, and Identity," *Sociological Review* 47, no. 1 (1999): 91–109.

33. James N. Rosenau, "Emergent Spaces, New Places, Old Faces: Proliferating Identities in a Globalizing World," in *Worlds on the Move: Globalization, Migration, and Cultural Security*, ed. Jonathan Friedman and Shalini Randeria (London: I. B. Tauris, 2004), 23–62.

34. An exchange between Stuart Hall and James Clifford teases out Hall's ideas of "dwelling-in-traveling" and "traveling-in-dwelling." James Clifford, "Traveling Cultures,"

in *Cultural Studies*, ed. Lawrence Grossberg, Cary Nelson, and Paula Treichler (New York: Routledge, 1992), 96–116.

35. Chawla and Jones, introduction to *Stories of Home*, xiii.

36. Ibid.

37. Sara Ahmed, "Home and Away: Narratives of Migration and Estrangement," *International Journal of Cultural Studies* 2, no. 3 (1999): 340.

38. Ibid.

39. Emily McKee, *Dwelling in Conflict: Negev Landscapes and the Boundaries of Belonging* (Stanford: Stanford University Press, 2016), 11. On "dwelling practices," see also Celia Lury, "The Objects of Travel," in *Touring Cultures: Transformations of Travel and Theory*, ed. Chris Rojek and John Urry (London: Routledge, 1997), 78.

40. McKee, *Dwelling in Conflict*, 11.

41. Nedra Reynolds, *Geographies of Writing: Inhabiting Places and Encountering Difference* (Carbondale: Southern Illinois Press, 2004), 140. Reynolds echoes Michel de Certeau who defined dwelling as an "everyday practice" in his book, *The Practice of Everyday Life* (Berkeley: University of California Press, 1984), xxi–xxii. Social theorists have drawn upon dwelling as a set of practices to explain the relationships between thinking, writing, and travel. See James Clifford, *Routes: Travel and Translation in the Late Twentieth Century* (Cambridge: Harvard University Press, 1997); Heidegger, "Building Dwelling Thinking."

42. Kathy-Ann Tan, *Reconfiguring Citizenship and National Identity in the North American Literary Imagination* (Detroit: Wayne State University Press, 2015), 196.

43. Mary H. Moran, *Civilized Women: Gender and Prestige in Southeastern Liberia* (Ithaca: Cornell University Press, 1990), 5.

44. Ahmed, "Home and Away."

45. Ibid., 336.

46. Emily McKee, *Dwelling in Conflict*, 11.

47. Ibid., 12.

48. Leymah Gbowee and Carol Mithers, *Mighty Be Our Powers: How Sisterhood, Prayer, and Sex Changed a Nation at War* (New York: Beast Books, 2011), 157. Subsequent references to this work, abbreviated *MBOP*, will appear parenthetically in the text.

49. Victoria Reffell of National Reconciliation Reunification Commission, helped organize the peace conference in Freetown, Sierra Leone, in 1990. She was only a part of the ad hoc peace initiative promoting the talks; Weade Kobbah Wureh, Director General of the Liberia Broadcasting System, observed a "lack of concern for the plight of the people and began to question the value of such meetings"; Myrtle Gibson and Muna Wreh attended the ECOWAS conference in Lomé, Togo, in February 1991 on their own and only circulated a paper about how war was affecting women and children most; and throughout 1991–93, women's organizations were not recognized as observers or as participants by ECOWAS or the UN.

50. Mary Louise Pratt, *Imperial Eyes: Travel Writing and Transculturation* (New York: Routledge, 1992); Tan, *Reconfiguring Citizenship*, 197.

51. Tan, *Reconfiguring Citizenship*, 197.

52. Susan Wittig Albert, *Together, Alone: A Memoir of Marriage and Place* (Austin: University of Texas Press, 2009), 54.

53. Mary H. Moran, "Our Mothers Have Spoken: Synthesizing Old and New Forms of Women's Political Authority in Liberia," *Journal of International Women's Studies* 13, no. 4 (2012): 51–66; Mary H. Moran and M. Anne Pitcher, "The 'Basket Case' and the 'Poster Child': Explaining the End of Civil Conflicts in Liberia and Mozambique," *Third World Quarterly* 25, no. 3 (2004): 501–19; Prasch, "Maternal Bodies."

54. Rosenau, "Emergent Spaces," xv.

55. For a thorough discussion of militant philosophies and strategies toward social change, see Southard, *Militant Citizenship*, 14–16, 63–64.

56. For an analysis focused solely on Gbowee's protest rhetoric, see Prasch, "Maternal Bodies."

57. Priscilla Hayner, "Negotiating Peace in Liberia: Preserving the Possibility for Justice," Henry Dunant Centre for Humanitarian Dialogue, November 2007, 5, 12. Available for download at https://www.ictj.org/sites/default/files/ICTJ-Liberia-Negotiating -Peace-2007-English_0.pdf.

58. Ibid.,12.

59. Theobald, *Role of Women*, 53.

60. Tamasin Ford, "Domestic Violence is Biggest Threat to West Africa's Women, IRC Says," *Guardian*, May 22, 2012, https://www.theguardian.com/global-development /2012/may/22/domestic-violence-west-africa-irc/; "Tackling Liberia's High Rape Rate," *IRIN News*, July 18, 2014, http://www.irinnews.org/report/100364/tackling-liberia's -high-rape-rate/.

CHAPTER 2

1. Human Rights Watch, "How to Fight, How to Kill: Child Soldiers in Liberia," February 2, 2004, 1. Retrieved from http://www.hrw.org/en/reports/2004/02/02/how -fight-how-kill/.

2. Ellen Johnson Sirleaf, *This Child Will Be Great: Memoir of a Remarkable Life by Africa's First Woman President* (New York: HarperCollins, 2009), 310, 312. Subsequent references to this work, abbreviated *TCWBG*, will appear parenthetically in the text.

3. Ellen Johnson Sirleaf, "Inaugural Address of H. E. Ellen Johnson Sirleaf," January 16, 2006, 12. The text of this speech and the speeches that follow can be found at Liberia's official site for the president, "The Executive Mansion," accessed January 8, 2016, http://www.emansion.gov.lr/2content_list_sub.php?main=24&related=24&pg= mp/. Speech titles are exactly as they appear on the pdf of each speech text.

4. Martha C. Nussbaum, "Patriotism and Cosmopolitanism," in *For Love of Country: Debating the Limits of Patriotism*, ed. Joshua Cohen (Boston: Beacon Press, 1996), 9.

5. Martha C. Nussbaum, "Toward a Globally Sensitive Patriotism," *Daedalus* 137, no. 3 (2008): 80.

6. Kwame Anthony Appiah, "Cosmopolitan Patriots," in Cohen, *For Love of Country*, 22.

7. Amy Gutman, "Democratic Citizenship," in Cohen, *For Love of Country*, 66–71.

8. Luis Cabrera, *The Practice of Global Citizenship* (Cambridge: Cambridge University Press, 2010), 3.

9. Barbara Arneil, "Global Citizenship versus Cosmopolitanism: Lessons Learned from Chinese Dissidents, Global Indigenous Peoples Movement, and the Convention on the Rights of People with Disabilities," in *Cosmopolitanism and the Legacies of Dissent*, ed. Tamara Caraus and Camil Alexandru Pârvu (New York: Routledge, 2015), 218.

10. Ibid., 218–19.

11. Ulrich Beck, *Cosmopolitan Vision*, trans. Ciaran Cronin (Cambridge: Polity Press, 2006), 49; Robert Post, introduction to *Another Cosmopolitanism* by Seyla Benhabib (Oxford: Oxford University Press, 2006), 4.

12. Beck, *Cosmopolitan Vision*, 49.

13. Ibid.

14. Kathleen Glenister Roberts, "Dialog Ethics, Cosmopolitanism, and Intercultural Communication," in *Communication Ethics: Between Cosmopolitanism and*

Provinciality, ed. Kathleen Glenister Roberts and Ronald C. Arnett (New York: Peter Lang, 2008), 90.

15. Ibid., 89–104. Also see the edited volume for more works on ethics, cosmopolitanism, and provinciality.

16. Gerard Delanty, *Citizenship in a Global Age: Society, Culture, Politics* (Buckingham, UK: Open University Press, 2000), 143.

17. With the exception of *Cosmopolitanism and the Legacies of Dissent*, ed. Tamara Caraus and Camil Alexandru Pârvu (New York: Routledge, 2015), which focuses less on "cosmopolitan citizenship" and more on how leaders of social change functioned as models of a cosmopolitan morality.

18. In the field of communication studies broadly, studies of cosmopolitan citizenship populate journals of intercultural communication and media and culture.

19. See, for example, Vanessa B. Beasley, ed., *Who Belongs in America?: Presidents, Rhetoric, Immigration* (College Station: Texas A&M University Press, 2006); David Josue Cisneros, *The Border Crossed Us: Rhetorics of Border, Citizenship, and Latino/a Identity* (Tuscaloosa: University of Alabama Press, 2013); Karma Chávez, "Border (In)Securities: Normative and Differential Belonging in LGBTQ and Immigrant Rights Discourse," *Communication and Critical/Cultural Studies* 7, no. 2 (2010): 136–55; and Sara L. McKinnon, "Positioned in/by the State: Incorporation, Exclusion, and Appropriation of Women's Gender-Based Claims to Political Asylum in the United States," *Quarterly Journal of Speech* 97, no. 2 (2011): 178–200.

20. Ronald C. Arnett, for example, examined the cosmopolitan and provincial aspects of a Barack Obama speech. Ronald C. Arnett, "Civic Rhetoric—Meeting the Communal Interplay of the Provincial and the Cosmopolitan: Barack Obama's Notre Dame Speech," *Rhetoric and Public Affairs* 14, no. 4 (2011): 631–71. See also Roberts and Arnett, eds., *Communication Ethics* (New York: Peter Lang, 2008).

21. J. Gus Liebenow, *Liberia: The Quest for Democracy* (Bloomington: Indiana University Press, 1987), 19.

22. Mary H. Moran, *Liberia: The Violence of Democracy* (Philadelphia: University of Pennsylvania Press, 2006), 2.

23. Benjamin G. Dennis and Anita K. Dennis, *Slaves to Racism: An Unbroken Chain from America to Liberia* (New York: Algora, 2008), 3.

24. Kenneth C. Omeje, "Introduction: Discourses of the Liberian Civil War and the Imperatives of Peacebuilding," in *War to Peace Transition: Conflict Intervention and Peacebuilding in Liberia*, ed. Kenneth C. Omeje (Lanham: University Press of America, 2009), 10.

25. United Nations Development Programme (UNDP), *Mobilizing Capacity for Reconstruction and Development*, National Human Development Report: Liberia 2006 (Monrovia: United Nations Development Programme, 2006), 42. Retrieved from http://hdr.undp.org/sites/default/files/liberia_2006_en.pdf.

26. Melinda Adams, "Liberia's Election of Ellen Johnson-Sirleaf and Women's Executive Leadership in Africa," *Politics and Gender* 4, no. 3 (2008): 480–81.

27. Ibid., 481–82.

28. Nussbaum, "Patriotism and Cosmopolitanism."

29. Gutman, "Democratic Citizenship," 69.

30. Ibid., 70.

31. Jay P. Childers, "Dislocated Cosmopolitans," chap. 3 in *The Evolving Citizen: American Youth and the Changing Norms of Democratic Engagement* (University Park: Pennsylvania State University Press, 2012), 54–84.

32. Veronika Fuest, "'This Is the Time to Get out in Front': Changing Roles and Opportunities for Women in Liberia," *African Affairs* 107, no. 427 (2008): 206.

33. Ibid.

34. Moran, *Liberia*, 90.

35. Ibid., 95.

36. Ibid., 82.

37. Fuest, "'This is the Time,'" 216–17.

38. Ellen Johnson Sirleaf, "Remarks by Her Excellency Ellen Johnson Sirleaf, President of the Republic of Liberia, European Development Day Forum, Brussels, Belgium," November 15, 2006, 4.

39. Ellen Johnson Sirleaf, "Intervention by H. E. President Ellen Johnson Sirleaf at Clinton Global Initiative's Panel Discussion on 'Empowering Girls and Women,' New York," September 21, 2010, 5.

40. Ellen Johnson Sirleaf, "Remarks by H. E. President Ellen Johnson Sirleaf at Official Signing Ceremony of the Education Reform Act of 2011, William V. S. Tubman High School, Sinkor," August 8, 2011, 3.

41. Ellen Johnson Sirleaf, "Inaugural Address of H. E. Ellen Johnson Sirleaf," January 16, 2006, 12.

42. Ellen Johnson Sirleaf, "Address by Her Excellency Ellen Johnson Sirleaf, President of the Republic of Liberia at the Opening Ceremony of the 2nd Meeting of 'Women for a Better World,' on the Occasion of International Women's Day," March 7, 2007, 6.

43. Sirleaf, "Opening Ceremony of 2nd Meeting," 8.

44. Ellen Johnson Sirleaf, "Annual Message to the Fourth Session of the 52nd National Legislature of the Republic by Her Excellency Ellen Johnson Sirleaf, President of the Republic of Liberia, Capitol Hill, Monrovia," January 26, 2008, 17.

45. Sirleaf, "Annual Message to the Fourth Session," 19. Sirleaf mentions anti-rape laws and other measures designed to punish violence against women in the following addresses: "Transcript of President Ellen Johnson Sirleaf's Statement During the Groundbreaking on Friday, June 5, 2009, for the Construction of a New United States of America Embassy Complex in Monrovia," June 5, 2009; "Annual Message to the Sixth Session of the 52nd National Legislature of the Republic of Liberia. Theme: Our Nation is Heading in the Right Direction," January 24, 2011; "Opening Ceremony of the 2nd Meeting of 'Women for a Better World'"; "European Development Day Forum"; "'Leadership to End World Hunger,' Remarks by Her Excellency Ellen Johnson Sirleaf, President of Liberia, On the Occasion of Receiving 2006 Africa Prize for Leadership Awarded by the Hunger Project," October 21, 2006; and "Goodwill Message by Her Excellency Ellen Johnson Sirleaf at the Official Program of International Women's Day," March 8, 2008.

46. Ellen Johnson Sirleaf, "Special Remarks by Her Excellency President Ellen Johnson Sirleaf, at Cross-Learning Initiative Conference on UN Security Council Resolution 1325," April 13, 2010, 16.

47. Sirleaf, "Annual Message to the Fourth Session," 18; Sirleaf, "Goodwill Message," 2; Ellen Johnson Sirleaf, "Annual Message to the Fifth Session of the 52nd National Legislature of the Republic of Liberia by Her Excellency Ellen Johnson Sirleaf," January 25, 2010, 75.

48. Sirleaf, "Goodwill Message," 3.

49. Sirleaf, "Opening Ceremony of 2nd Meeting," 5.

50. Ibid., 10.

51. Benhabib, *Another Cosmopolitanism*, 20.

52. Cabrera, *Practice of Global Citizenship*, 3–4.

53. The complex relationship between rhetoric, policy change, and shared social norms cannot fully be discussed here, but for a concise sketch, see Celeste Michelle Condit, *Decoding Abortion Rhetoric: Communicating Social Change* (Urbana: University of Illinois, 1990), 1–12.

54. Moran, *Liberia*, 40–48; Caroline Bledsoe, *Women and Marriage in Kpelle Society* (Stanford: Stanford University Press, 1980), 110.

55. Stanton Peabody, "Women Who Made a Difference," *Liberian Studies Journal* 31, no. 1 (2006): 63–89; Worldwide Guide to Women in Leadership, accessed April 16, 2015, http://www.guide2womenleaders.com/womeninpower/Africa.htm.

56. Inter-Parliamentary Union, "Women in National Parliaments," accessed June 26, 2015, http://www.ipu.org/wmn-e/arc/world010615.htm.

57. Worldwide Guide to Women in Leadership.

58. Aili Mari Tripp, "The Evolution of Transnational Feminisms: Consensus, Conflict, and New Dynamics," in *Global Feminism*, ed. Myra Marx Ferree and Aili Mari Tripp (New York: New York University Press, 2006), 67.

59. Ibid.

60. Ellen Johnson Sirleaf, "Keynote Address by H. E. Ellen Johnson Sirleaf, President of the Republic of Liberia at the International Women Leaders' Conference on 'Women's Leadership for Sustainable Development,' Jerusalem and Haifa, Israel," November 18, 2007, 1, 3.

61. Ellen Johnson Sirleaf, "Keynote Address by Her Excellency Ellen Johnson Sirleaf President of the Republic of Liberia at the United Nations Institute for Training and Research Torino Retreat," August 31, 2007, 6.

62. Ellen Johnson Sirleaf, "'African Women and Political Participation,' Lecture by H. E. Ellen Johnson Sirleaf, President of the Republic of Liberia on the Occasion of the 10th Anniversary of the African Women's Development Fund (AWDF), Accra, Ghana," November 12, 2010, 9.

63. Ellen Johnson Sirleaf, "Remarks by H. E. President Ellen Johnson Sirleaf at Community of Democracies/Council of Women World Leaders Panel Discussion on 'Women as a Critical Force in Democratic Governance,'" September 23, 2010, 1.

64. Sirleaf, "'African Women and Political Participation,'" 2.

65. Ellen Johnson Sirleaf, "Opening Remarks by Her Excellency Ellen Johnson Sirleaf, President of the Republic of Liberia at the International Spain-Africa Meeting, Women for a Better World," Valencia, Spain, March 27, 2010, 3.

66. Sirleaf, "Community of Democracies," 3; Sirleaf, "'African Women and Political Participation,'" 5.

67. Ellen Johnson Sirleaf, "Keynote Address by H. E. President Ellen Johnson on 'Liberian Women's Involvement in Peacemaking and Peacebuilding,' in International Peace Institute's African Leaders Series: Consolidating a Future in Peace, New York," September 26, 2012, 3.

68. Ellen Johnson Sirleaf, "Statement by H. E. President Ellen Johnson Sirleaf at Launch of the Joint Global Program on Economic Empowerment for Rural Women," September 27, 2012, 2.

69. Sirleaf, "Joint Global Program," 2.

70. Ellen Johnson Sirleaf, "Keynote Address by Her Excellency Ellen Johnson Sirleaf, President of the Republic of Liberia at First Meeting of the Africa Commission," April 16, 2008, 7.

71. Sirleaf, "First Meeting of Africa Commission," 7.

72. Ellen Johnson Sirleaf, "Speech Delivered by Her Excellency Ellen Johnson Sirleaf, President of the Republic of Liberia at the 95th International Labour Conference," June 7, 2006, 1.

73. Sirleaf, "International Women Leaders' Conference," 3.

74. Ibid.

75. Ibid.

76. Ibid., 1.

77. Sirleaf, "Community of Democracies," 3.

78. James D. Ingram, *Radical Cosmopolitics: The Ethics and Politics of Democratic Universalism* (New York: Columbia University Press, 2013), 35; Appiah, "Cosmopolitan Patriots," 22.

79. Ulrike M. Vieten, *Gender and Cosmopolitanism in Europe: A Feminist Perspective* (Surrey, UK: Ashgate, 2012); Pnina Werbner, "Introduction: Towards a New Cosmopolitan Anthropology," in *Anthropology and the New Cosmopolitanism: Rooted, Feminist, and Vernacular Perspectives*, ed. Pnina Werbner (Oxford: Berg, 2008), 2.

80. Nancy A. Naples and Manisha Desai, eds., *Women's Activism and Globalization: Linking Local Struggles and Transnational Politics* (New York: Routledge, 2002).

81. See Gracia Clark, *Onions Are My Husband: Survival and Accumulation by West African Market Women* (Chicago: University of Chicago Press, 1994).

82. Helene Cooper, *Madame President: The Extraordinary Journey of Ellen Johnson Sirleaf* (New York: Simon and Schuster, 2017), 179.

83. Ibid.

84. Ellen Johnson Sirleaf, "Statement by H. E. President Ellen Johnson Sirleaf at World Premiere of the Sirleaf Market Women's Fund Video Documentary and Case Study: *God First, Second the Market: The Story of the Sirleaf Market Women's Fund of Liberia*," August 23, 2012, 3.

85. Sirleaf, "Market Women's Fund Video," 1.

86. Ellen Johnson Sirleaf, "Keynote Address by H. E. President Ellen Johnson Sirleaf at World Bank Seminar on 'Women in the Private Sector: Good for Development and Business,'" Tokyo International Forum, October 11, 2012, 3.

87. Ellen Johnson Sirleaf, "Address by Her Excellency Ellen Johnson Sirleaf, President of the Republic of Liberia on the Occasion of the 45th Commencement of Cuttington University," July 9, 2006, 4.

88. Ellen Johnson Sirleaf, "Address by H. E. President Ellen Johnson Sirleaf at the 17th Convocation of the University of Agriculture at Abeokuta," February 18, 2010, 3.

89. See, for example, Rebecca Dingo, *Networking Arguments: Rhetoric, Transnational Feminism, and Public Policy Writing* (Pittsburgh: University of Pittsburgh Press, 2012); Rebecca Dingo and J. Blake Scott, eds., *The Megarhetorics of Global Development* (Pittsburgh: University of Pittsburgh Press, 2012); and Winnie Woodhull, "Global Feminisms, Transnational Political Economies, Third World Cultural Production," *Journal of International Women's Studies* 4, no. 2 (2003): 76–90.

90. Sirleaf, "Market Women's Fund Video," 3; Sirleaf, "'African Women and Political Participation,'" 2.

91. Clinton Foundation, "Our Work: Girls and Women," accessed October 20, 2017, https://www.clintonfoundation.org/our-work/by-topic/girls-and-women/.

92. Sirleaf, "'African Women and Political Participation,'" 2.

93. Sirleaf, "Intervention," 2.

94. Sirleaf, "Market Women's Fund Video," 4.

95. Sirleaf, "Launch of Joint Global Program," 3–4.

96. Sirleaf, "Market Women's Fund Video," 4.

97. Sirleaf, "'Women in the Private Sector'" 3, 4.

98. Ellen Johnson Sirleaf, "Statement by H. E. President Ellen Johnson Sirleaf at Goldman Sachs/CHF 10,000 Women Graduation Ceremony, Monrovia City Hall," February 10, 2012, 3.

99. Ellen Johnson Sirleaf, "Keynote Remarks by H. E. President Ellen Johnson Sirleaf at Graduation for Goldman Sachs 10,000 Women Project," December 3, 2010, 8.

100. Ibid., 2–3.

101. Ibid.

102. Ellen Johnson Sirleaf, "'Behold the New Africa,' Sixth Nelson Mandela Annual Lecture, 2008," July 12, 2008, 5.

103. Ellen Johnson Sirleaf, "Statement by Her Excellency Madam Ellen Johnson Sirleaf, President of the Republic of Liberia at State Dinner in Honour of his Excellency Mr. John Aygekum Kufuor, President of the Republic of Ghana, Monrovia, Liberia," November 22, 2008, 2.

104. Vieten, *Gender and Cosmopolitanism*, 3.

105. Gwendolyn S. Myers, "Dialogue Among Peace Messengers: Conditions of Liberian Women; A Political Dimension," *Daily Observer*, April 21, 2016.

106. UN Women, "Women Police Making Strides Across Africa," *The World Post*, April 14, 2016.

107. Alex Pearlman, "No Liberty for Liberian Women as Rapes Continue," *Global Post*, September 21, 2012.

108. Michal Zebede and Shiza Shahid, "Liberia's 'Sex4Grades' Epidemic is Ruining Children's Lives," *Time*, April 5, 2016.

109. Cooper, *Madame President*, 238.

110. Ibid., 239.

111. Ibid., 240.

112. Ibid., 222.

113. Ibid., 222, 237.

114. Teresa Wiltz, "Feminism's Vital Role in Rebuilding Liberia," *The Root*, December 24, 2010.

115. Tamasin Ford, "Wronged Women of Liberia Reluctant to Revisit Human Rights Abuses," *Guardian*, February 28, 2012.

116. Saint Louis Chapter of Amnesty International, "23 Fast Facts about Women's Oppression Worldwide," accessed January 1, 2016, https://amnestystlouis.wordpress .com/2013/06/17/23-fast-facts-about-womens-oppression-worldwide/; UN Secretary-General's Campaign: United to End the Violence Against Women, United Nations, "Human Rights Violation," accessed January 1, 2016, http://endviolence.un.org/situa tion.shtml.

117. Werbner, "Introduction," 18.

118. Vieten, *Gender and Cosmopolitanism*, 4.

CHAPTER 3

1. Doris H. Railey, "Some Impacts of the Liberian Civil War: A Pilot Study of Thirty Liberian Immigrant Families in the United States," *Liberian Studies Journal* 22, no. 2 (1997): 261.

2. Rebecca Dingo, *Networking Arguments: Rhetoric, Transnational Feminism, and Public Policy Writing* (Pittsburgh: University of Pittsburgh Press, 2011), 3.

3. Inderpal Grewal, "'Women's Rights as Human Rights': Feminist Practices, Global Feminism, and Human Rights Regimes in Transnationality," *Citizenship Studies* 3, no. 3 (1999): 337–54.

4. Anne Sisson Runyan, "Global Feminism," in *Feminism and Women's Rights Worldwide*, ed. Michele A. Paludi (Santa Barbara, CA: Praeger, 2010), 8.

5. Wendy S. Hesford and Eileen E. Schell, "Configurations of Transnationality: Locating Feminist Rhetorics," *College English* 70, no. 5 (2008): 461–70.

6. Nancy A. Naples, "The Challenges and Possibilities of Transnational Feminist Praxis," in *Women's Activism and Globalization: Linking Local Struggles and Transnational Politics*, ed. Nancy A. Naples and Manisha Desai (New York: Routledge, 2002), 267; Raka

Shome, "Transnational Feminism in Communication Studies," *The Communication Review* 9, no. 4 (2006): 257.

7. Aihwa Ong, *Flexible Citizenship: The Cultural Logics of Transnationality* (Durham: Duke University Press, 1999), 4.

8. J. Blake Scott and Rebecca Dingo, introduction to *The Megarhetorics of Global Development*, ed. Rebecca Dingo and J. Blake Scott (Pittsburgh: University of Pittsburgh Press, 2012), 7.

9. Dingo, *Networking Arguments*.

10. Rebecca S. Richards, *Transnational Feminist Rhetorics and Gendered Leadership: From Daughters of Destiny to Iron Ladies* (Lanham: Lexington Books, 2015).

11. Wendy S. Hesford, "Global Turns and Cautions in Rhetoric and Composition Studies," *PMLA* 121, no. 3 (2006): 787–801.

12. Sara McKinnon, "(In)Hospitable Publics: Theorizing Modalities of Access to US Publics," in *Public Modalities: Rhetoric, Culture, Media, and the Shape of Public Life*, ed. Daniel C. Brower and Robert Asen (Tuscaloosa: University of Alabama Press, 2010), 131–53.

13. Inderpal Grewal, *Transnational America: Feminisms, Diasporas, Neoliberalisms* (Durham: Duke University Press, 2005), 3.

14. Rebecca Dingo, introduction to Richards, *Transnational Feminist Rhetorics*, ix.

15. Hesford, "Global Turns," 794.

16. Nancy Naples and Manisha Desai, preface to Naples and Desai, *Women's Activism and Globalization*, xii.

17. Myra Marx Ferree and Aili Mari Tripp, preface to *Global Feminism: Transnational Women's Activism, Organizing, and Human Rights*, ed. Myra Marx Ferree and Aili Mari Tripp (New York: New York University Press, 2006), viii.

18. Anne Sisson Runyan, "Global Feminism," 8–9.

19. Ferree and Tripp, preface, vii.

20. Arabella Lyon, *Deliberative Acts: Democracy, Rhetoric, and Rights* (University Park: Pennsylvania State University Press, 2015), 69.

21. "About UN Women," UN Women, accessed October 5, 2015, http://www.unwomen.org/en/about-us/about-un-women/.

22. Gayle Tzemach Lemmon, "Michelle Bachelet Has a Mission to Help the World's Women," *Newsweek*, September 12, 2011, 7–8.

23. Robert Falkner, Hannes Stephan, and John Vogler, "International Climate Policy after Copenhagen: Toward a 'Building Blocks' Approach," *Global Policy* 3 (2010): 252–62.

24. Thomas G. Weiss and Ramesh Shakur, *Global Governance and the UN: An Unfinished Journey* (Bloomington: Indiana University Press, 2010).

25. Margaret E. Keck and Kathryn Sikkink, *Activists Beyond Borders: Advocacy Networks in International Politics* (Ithaca: Cornell University Press, 1998), 1.

26. Ibid., 2.

27. Ibid.

28. Ibid., 12.

29. "Short History of the Commission on the Status of Women," UN Women, accessed October 15, 2015. Available for download at http://www.un.org/womenwatch/daw/CSW60YRS/CSWbriefhistory.pdf.

30. "About UN Women."

31. Gwynn Thomas and Melinda Adams, "Breaking the Final Glass Ceiling: The Influence of Gender in the Elections of Ellen Johnson Sirleaf and Michelle Bachelet," *Journal of Women, Politics, and Policy* 31, no. 2 (2010): 119–20.

32. Ibid.

33. Lemmon, "Michelle Bachelet," 7–8.

34. Alfonso Daniels, "From Torture Victim to President," *Progressive* 70, no. 3 (2006): 30–32.

35. Gwynn Thomas, "Bachelet's Liderazgo Femenino (Feminine Leadership)," *International Feminist Journal of Politics* 13, no. 1 (2011): 63–82.

36. Thomas and Adams, "Final Glass Ceiling," 123.

37. Gregory Weeks and Silvia Borzutzy, "Michelle Bachelet's Government: The Paradoxes of a Chilean President," *Journal of Politics in Latin America* 4, no. 3 (2012): 106–7.

38. Emily A. Haddad and William E. Schweinle, "The Feminine Political Persona: Queen Victoria, Ellen Johnson Sirleaf, and Michelle Bachelet," in *Women and Management: Global Issues and Promising Solutions*, ed. Michele A. Paludi (Santa Barbara, CA: Praeger, 2013), 317.

39. Susan Franceschet, "Continuity or Change?: Gender Policy in the Bachelet Administration," in *The Bachelet Government: Conflict and Consensus in Post-Pinochet Chile*, ed. Silvia Borzutzy and Gregory B. Weeks (Gainesville: University Press of Florida, 2010), 158–80.

40. Susan Franceschet, "Gender Policy in the Bachelet Administration," in Borzutzy and Weeks, *The Bachelet Government*, 173.

41. "Bachelet Is Back," *Economist*. Web. April 6, 2013. Accessed April 3, 2018, https://www.economist.com/news/americas/21575806-not-quite-shoo-she-looks -bachelet-back/.

42. This chapter follows Lloyd F. Bitzer's notion of the rhetorical situation insofar as "the presence of rhetorical discourse obviously indicated the presence of a rhetorical situation." See Lloyd F. Bitzer, "The Rhetorical Situation," *Philosophy and Rhetoric* 1 (1968): 1. In this case, I find that Bachelet constructed a rhetorical situation through strategic choices in her discourse. In this sense, her discourse is emblematic of Richard Vatz's argument that rhetorical situations can be constructed and therefore certain elements are more "present" or "salient." See Richard E. Vatz, "The Myth of the Rhetorical Situation," *Philosophy and Rhetoric* 6, no. 3 (1973): 154–61.

43. Chaïm Perelman and L. Olbrechts-Tyteca, *The New Rhetoric: A Treatise on Argumentation*, trans. John Wilkinson and Purcell Weaver (Notre Dame: University of Notre Dame Press, 1969), 142.

44. Ibid., 115–20.

45. Michelle Bachelet, "Speech by Michelle Bachelet at the NGO CSW Forum Consultation Day" (presentation, NGO CSW Forum Consultation Day, New York, NY, March 3, 2013). Available at http://www.unwomen.org/en/news/stories/2013/3/speech -by-michelle-bachelet-at-the-ngo-csw-forum-consultation-day/.

46. Catherine Helen Palczewski, "Survivor Testimony in the Pornography Industry: Assessing Credibility in the Minneapolis Hearings and the Attorney General's Report," in *Warranting Assent: Case Studies in Argument Evaluation*, ed. Edward Schiappa (Albany: State University of New York, 1995), 276.

47. Ibid., 257–81; Barbara A. Pickering, "Women's Voices as Evidence: Personal Testimony in Pro-choice Films," *Argumentation and Advocacy* 40 (2003): 1–22.

48. Michelle Bachelet, "Access to Clean Energy Critical for Rural Women" (presentation, Climate Change and Access to Energy CSW Side Event, New York, NY, March 5, 2012). Available at http://www.unwomen.org/en/news/stories/2012/3/access-to-clean -energy-critical-for-rural-women/.

49. Antonyia Parvanova, "Survivors' Forum" (Special event organized by the United Nations Entity for Gender Equality and the Empowerment of Women [UN Women,] New York, NY, December 13, 2012). Available at http://webtv.un.org/news-features/add-your -voice-series/watch/survivors'-forum/2033921053001/.

50. Maria da Penha, "Survivors' Forum" (special event organized by the United Nations Entity for Gender Equality and the Empowerment of Women [UN Women], New York, NY, December 13, 2012). Available at http://webtv.un.org/news-features/add -your-voice-series/watch/survivors'-forum/2033921053001/.

51. Ibid.

52. Ibid.

53. Elora Halim Chowdhury, *Transnationalism Reversed: Women Organizing Against Violence in Bangladesh* (Albany: SUNY Press, 2011), xviii. See also Wendy S. Hesford, *Spectacular Rhetorics: Human Rights Visions, Recognitions, Feminisms* (Durham: Duke University Press, 2011).

54. Michelle Bachelet, "Opening Statement of Michelle Bachelet at CSW57: 'Time for Action: Prevent and End Violence Against Women and Girls,'" (presentation, 57th Session on UN Commission on the Status of Women, New York, NY, March 4, 2013). Available at http://www.unwomen.org/en/news/stories/2013/3/opening-statement-of -michelle-bachelet-at-csw57/.

55. Ibid.

56. Pickering, "Women's Voices as Evidence," 20.

57. Gayatri Spivak, "Can the Subaltern Speak? Speculations on Widow Sacrifice," *Wedge* 7–8 (Winter–Spring 1985): 120–30.

58. Bachelet, "Time for Action."

59. Bachelet, "Speech by Michelle Bachelet at the NGO CSW Forum."

60. Michal Givoni, *The Care of the Witness: A Contemporary History of Testimony in Crises* (Cambridge: Cambridge University Press, 2016), 11.

61. Shoshana Felman and Dori Laub, *Testimony: Crises of Witnessing in Literature, Psychoanalysis, and History* (New York: Routledge, 1992), 70–71.

62. Govani, *Care of the Witness*, 12.

63. Karlyn Kohrs Campbell, "Consciousness-Raising: Linking Theory, Criticism, and Practice," *Rhetoric Society Quarterly* 32, no. 1 (2002): 45–64; Kristina Horn Sheeler and Karrin Vasby Anderson, "Gender, Rhetoric, and International Political Systems: Angela Merkel's Negotiation of Proportional Representation and Party Politics," *Communication Quarterly* 62, no. 4 (2014): 474–95.

64. Susan Bickford, *The Dissonance of Democracy: Listening, Conflict, and Citizenship* (Ithaca: Cornell University Press, 1996), 97.

65. Kate Lacey, *Listening Publics: The Politics and Experience of Listening in the Media Age* (Cambridge: Polity Press, 2013), 163.

66. Krista Ratcliffe, *Rhetorical Listening: Identification, Gender, Whiteness* (Carbondale: Southern Illinois University Press, 2005), 19.

67. Michelle Bachelet, "Remarks by Michelle Bachelet on the Occasion of the Official Commemoration of the International Day to Eliminate Violence Against Women. A Promise is a Promise" (presentation, Official Commemoration of the International Day to Eliminate Violence Against Women, New York, NY, November 28, 2012). Available at http://www.unwomen.org/en/news/stories/2012/11/remarks-by-michelle-bachelet-on -the-occasion-of-the-official-commemoration-of-the-international-day/. Emphasis mine.

68. Bachelet, "Eliminate Violence Against Women."

69. Ibid.

70. Arabella Lyon and Lester C. Olson, "Human Rights Rhetoric: Traditions of Testifying and Witnessing," *Rhetoric Society Quarterly* 41, no. 3 (2011): 208.

71. Ibid.

72. Michelle Bachelet, "International Women's Day 2011: Time to Make the Promise of Equality a Reality," press release, March 8, 2011. Available at http://www

.unwomen.org/en/news/stories/2011/3/international-women-s-day-2011-time-to-make
-the-promise-of-equality-a-reality/.

73. Ibid., 4–5.

74. Ibid., 5.

75. Govani, *Care of the Witness*, 11.

76. Michelle Bachelet, "Press Statement by Michelle Bachelet at First Press Conference for CSW57" (presentation, 57th Session on the Commission on the Status of Women,
New York, NY, March 4, 2013). Available at http://www.unwomen.org/en/news/stories
/2013/3/press-statement-by-michelle-bachelet-at-first-press-conference-for-csw57/.

77. Bachelet, "Speech by Michelle Bachelet at the NGO CSW Forum."

78. Michelle Bachelet, "Michelle Bachelet's Closing Statement at the 57th Session
of the Commission on the Status of Women" (presentation, 57th Session on the Commission on the Status of Women, New York, NY, March 16, 2013). Available at http://
www.unwomen.org/en/news/stories/2013/3/michelle-bachelet-closing-statement-at
-the-57th-session-of-the-commission-on-the-status-of-women/.

79. Michelle Bachelet, "Remarks of Michelle Bachelet at the International Women's
Day Commemorative Event at the United Nations" (presentation, International Wom-
en's Day Commemorative Event at the United Nations, New York, NY, March 8, 2013).
Available at http://www.unwomen.org/en/news/stories/2013/3/remarks-of-michelle
-bachelet-at-the-international-womens-day-commemorative-event/.

80. Michelle Bachelet, "The Century of Inclusion and Women's Full Participation" (presentation, Kapuscinski Development Lectures, Dublin, Ireland, February 21,
2013). Available at http://www.unwomen.org/en/news/stories/2013/2/the-century-of
-inclusion-and-womens-full-participation/.

81. Ibid.

82. Ibid.

83. Ibid.

84. Ibid.

85. Bachelet, "International Women's Day."

86. Bachelet, "Century of Inclusion."

87. Michelle Bachelet, "The 56th Session of the Commission on the Status of
Women Is an Opportunity for Rural Women's Voices to Be Heard by Policy Makers"
(presentation, NGO CSW Forum Consultation Day, New York, NY, February 26, 2012).
Available at http://www.unwomen.org/en/news/stories/2012/2/the-56th-session-of-the
-commission-on-the-status-of-women-is-an-opportunity-for-rural-women-s-voices/.

88. Ibid.

89. Michelle Bachelet, "Introductory Statement by Ms. Michelle Bachelet—56th Session of the Commission on the Status of Women" (presentation, 56th Session of the Commission on the Status of Women, New York, NY, February 27, 2012). Available at http://
www.unwomen.org/en/news/stories/2012/2/introductory-statement-by-ms-michelle
-bachelet-56th-session-of-the-commission-on-the-status-of-wo/.

90. Bachelet, "Century of Inclusion."

91. Bachelet, "Speech by Michelle Bachelet at the NGO CSW Forum."

92. Michelle Bachelet, "Press Statement."

93. Aristotle's definition of the epideictic says its "business" is to "praise or blame,
its time the present (sometimes the past or the future), its end the noble or the disgrace-
ful." Aristotle, *Rhetoric*, xxxviii.

94. Celeste Michelle Condit, "The Functions of Epideictic: The Boston Massacre
Orations as Exemplar," *Communication Quarterly* 33, no. 4 (1985): 284–98.

95. Michelle Bachelet, "Michelle Bachelet's Closing Statement."

96. Bachelet, "Speech at the NGO CSW Forum Consultation Day." Emphasis mine.

97. James C. Franklin, "Shame on You: The Impact of Human Rights Criticism on Political Repression in Latin America," *International Studies Quarterly* 52, no. 1 (2008): 187–211; Emilie M. Hafner-Burton, "Sticks and Stones: Naming and Shaming the Human Rights Enforcement Problem," *International Organization* 62, no. 4 (2008): 689–716; James H. Lebovic and Eric Voeten, "The Politics of Shame: The Condemnation of Country Human Rights Practices in the UNHCR," *International Studies Quarterly* 50, no. 4 (2006): 861–88.

98. Michelle Bachelet, "Closing Remarks of Michelle Bachelet Under Secretary General and Executive Director of UN Women at Stakeholders' Forum on Preventing and Eliminating Violence Against Women" (presentation, Stakeholders' Forum on Preventing and Eliminating Violence Against Women, New York, NY, December 14, 2012). Available at http://www.unwomen.org/en/news/stories/2012/12/closing-remarks-of -michelle-bachelet-under-secretary-general-and-executive-director-of-un-women-at-s/. Emphasis mine.

99. Bachelet, "Press Statement."

100. Michelle Bachelet and Julia Duncan Cassell, "Presentation by Michelle Bachelet and Julia Duncan Cassell at a Side Event on the COMMIT Initiative" (presentation, Side Event on the COMMIT Initiative, New York, NY, March 5, 2013). Available at http://www .unwomen.org/en/news/stories/2013/3/presentation-by-michelle-bachelet-and-julia -duncan-cassell-at-a-side-event-on-the-commit-initiative/.

101. Bachelet, "International Women's Day."

102. Hesford, "Global Turns," 792.

103. Michelle Ballif, *Seduction, Sophistry, and the Woman with the Rhetorical Figure* (Carbondale: University of Southern Illinois Press, 2000), 9.

104. Bonnie J. Dow and Mari Boor Tonn, "'Feminine Style' and Political Judgment in the Rhetoric of Ann Richards," *Quarterly Journal of Speech* 79 (1993): 286–303; Susan Jarratt and Lynn Worsham, eds., *Feminism and Composition Studies: In Other Words* (New York: Modern Language Association, 1998); Louise Wetherbee Phelps and Janet Emig, eds., *Feminine Principles and Women's Experiences in American Composition and Rhetoric* (Pittsburgh: University of Pittsburgh Press, 1995); Sheeler and Anderson, "Gender, Rhetoric, and International Political Systems."

105. Karlyn Kohrs Campbell, "The Rhetoric of Women's Liberation: An Oxymoron," *Quarterly Journal of Speech* 59 (1973): 74–86; Dow and Tonn, "'Feminine Style' and Political Judgment."

CONCLUSION

1. Alexandra Dobrowolsky and Evangelia Tastsoglou, "Crossing Boundaries and Making Connections," in *Women, Migration, and Citizenship: Making Local, National, and Transnational Connections*, ed. Evangelia Tastsoglou and Alexandra Dobrowolsky (Burlington, VT: Ashgate, 2006), 4.

2. Thomas Rickert, *Ambient Rhetoric: The Attunements of Rhetorical Being* (Pittsburgh: University of Pittsburgh Press, 2013), 248.

3. Rebecca Dingo, *Networking Arguments: Rhetoric, Transnational Feminism, and Public Policy Writing* (Pittsburgh: University of Pittsburgh Press, 2012).

BIBLIOGRAPHY

Adams, Melinda. "Liberia's Election of Ellen Johnson-Sirleaf and Women's Executive Leadership in Africa." *Politics and Gender* 4, no. 3 (2008): 475–84.

Adebajo, Adekeye. *Building Peace in West Africa: Liberia, Sierra Leone, and Guinea-Bissau.* Boulder: Lynne Rienner, 2002.

Adler, K. H. "Gendering Histories of Homes and Homecomings." *Gender and History* 21, no. 3 (2009): 455–64.

African Women and Peace Support Group. *Liberian Women Peacemakers: Fighting for the Right to Be Seen, Heard, and Counted.* Trenton: Africa World Press, 2004.

Ahmed, Sara. "Home and Away: Narratives of Migration and Estrangement." *International Journal of Cultural Studies* 2, no. 3 (1999): 329–47.

Akanle, Olayinka. *Kinship Networks and International Migration in Nigeria.* Newcastle upon Tyne: Cambridge Scholars, 2013.

Albert, Susan Wittig. *Together, Alone: A Memoir of Marriage and Place.* Austin: University of Texas Press, 2009.

Allen, Danielle. *Talking to Strangers: Anxieties of Citizenship Since Brown v. Board of Education.* Chicago: University of Chicago Press, 2004.

Amaya, Hector. *Citizenship Excess: Latino/as, Media, and the Nation.* New York: New York University Press, 2013.

Anderson, Benedict. *Imagined Communities: Reflections on the Origin and Spread of Nationalism.* London: Verso, 2006.

Appiah, Kwame Anthony. "Cosmopolitan Patriots." In *For Love of Country: Debating the Limits of Patriotism,* edited by Joshua Cohen, 21–29. Boston: Beacon Press, 1996.

Aristotle. *The "Art" of Rhetoric.* Translated by John Henry Freese. Cambridge: Harvard University Press, 1975.

———. *The Politics.* Edited by E. H. Warmington. Cambridge: Harvard University Press, 1972.

Arne, James Aunt, and Enríque D. Rigsby, eds. *Civil Rights Rhetoric and the American Presidency.* College Station: Texas A&M University Press, 2005.

Arneil, Barbara. "Global Citizenship versus Cosmopolitanism: Lessons Learned from Chinese Dissidents, Global Indigenous Peoples Movement, and the Convention on the Rights of People with Disabilities." In *Cosmopolitanism and the Legacies of Dissent,* edited by Tamara Caraus and Camil Alexandru Pârvu, 214–33. New York: Routledge, 2015.

Arnett, Ronald C. "Civic Rhetoric—Meeting the Communal Interplay of the Provincial and the Cosmopolitan: Barack Obama's Notre Dame Speech." *Rhetoric and Public Affairs* 14, no. 4 (2011): 631–71.

Arthur, John A. *African Women Immigrants in the United States: Crossing Transnational Borders.* New York: Palgrave Macmillan, 2009.

Asen, Robert A. "A Discourse Theory of Citizenship." *Quarterly Journal of Speech* 90, no. 2 (2004): 189–211.

Atikcan, Ece Ozlem. "Citizenship or Denizenship: The Treatment of Third Country Nationals in the European Union." SEI Working Paper 85. Brighton: Sussex European Institute, 2006.

Aydinli, Ersel, and James N. Rosenau, eds. *Globalization, Security, and the Nation State: Paradigms in Transition*. Albany: SUNY Press, 2005.

"Bachelet Is Back." *Economist*, April 6, 2013.

Ballif, Michelle. *Seduction, Sophistry, and the Woman with the Rhetorical Figure*. Carbondale: University of Southern Illinois Press, 2000.

Beasley, Vanessa B. *You, the People: American National Identity in Presidential Rhetoric*. College Station: Texas A&M University Press, 2004.

Beck, Ulrich. *Cosmopolitan Vision*. Translated by Ciaran Cronin. Cambridge: Polity Press, 2006.

Behar, Ruth. Foreword to *Women on the Verge of Home*, edited by Bilinda Straight, ix–xi. Albany: SUNY Press, 2005.

Beneria, Lourdes, Günseli Berik, and Maria Floro, eds. *Gender, Development, and Globalization: Economics As If All People Mattered*. New York: Routledge, 2003.

Benhabib, Seyla. *Another Cosmopolitanism*. Oxford: Oxford University Press, 2006.

Bhabha, Homi K. *The Location of Culture*. London: Routledge, 1994.

Bickford, Susan. *The Dissonance of Democracy: Listening, Conflict, and Citizenship*. Ithaca: Cornell University Press, 1996.

Bitzer, Lloyd F. "The Rhetorical Situation." *Philosophy and Rhetoric* 1 (1968): 1–14.

Black, Jason Edward. *American Indians and the Rhetoric of Removal and Allotment*. Jackson: University of Mississippi Press, 2015.

Bledsoe, Caroline. *Women and Marriage in Kpelle Society*. Stanford: Stanford University Press, 1980.

Brandzel, Amy L. *Against Citizenship: The Violence of the Normative*. Urbana: University of Illinois Press, 2016.

Bruner, Michael Lane. "Global Governance and the Critical Public." *Rhetoric and Public Affairs* 6, no. 4 (2003): 687–708.

Buff, Rachel Ida. "Denizenship as Transnational Practice: Im/migration, Citizenship, and Empire in and around the Post-1945 U.S." In *The Transformation of Public Culture: Assessing the Politics of Diversity, Democracy, and Community in the United States, 1890 to the Present*, edited by Marguerite Shaffer, 263–72. Philadelphia: University of Pennsylvania Press, 2008.

Burke, Kenneth. *Gender Trouble: Feminism and the Subversion of Identity*. New York: Routledge, 1990.

———. *The Philosophy of Literary Form: Studies in Symbolic Action*. Berkeley: University of California Press, 1973.

———. *A Rhetoric of Motives*. Berkeley: University of California Press, 1969.

Butler, Judith. *Bodies that Matter: On the Discursive Limits of "Sex."* New York: Routledge, 1993.

Cabrera, Luis. *The Practice of Global Citizenship*. Cambridge: Cambridge University Press, 2010.

Campbell, John Angus. "Between the Fragment and the Icon: Prospect for a Rhetorical House of the Middle Way." *Western Journal of Speech Communication* 54, no. 3 (1990): 346–76.

Campbell, Karlyn Kohrs. "Agency: Promiscuous and Protean." *Communication and Critical/Cultural Studies* 2, no. 1 (2005): 1–19.

———. "Consciousness-Raising: Linking Theory, Criticism, and Practice." *Rhetoric Society Quarterly* 32, no. 1 (2002): 45–64.

———. *Man Cannot Speak for Her*. Vol. 1, *A Critical Study of Early Feminist Rhetoric*. New York: Praeger, 1989.

———. *Man Cannot Speak for Her*. Vol. 2, *Key Texts of the Early Feminists*. New York: Praeger, 1989.

———. "The Rhetoric of Women's Liberation: An Oxymoron." *Quarterly Journal of Speech* 59 (1973): 74–86.

Certeau, Michel de. *The Practice of Everyday Life.* Berkeley: University of California Press, 1984.

Chávez, Karma. "Border (In)Securities: Normative and Differential Belonging in LGBTQ and Immigrant Rights Discourses." *Communication and Critical/Cultural Studies* 7, no. 2 (2010): 136–55.

———. *Queer Migration Politics: Activist Rhetoric and Coalitional Possibilities.* Urbana: University of Illinois Press, 2013.

Chawla, Devika, and Stacy Holman Jones. Introduction to *Stories of Home: Place, Identity, Exile,* edited by Devika Chawla and Stacy Holman Jones, xi–xxiii. Lanham: Lexington Books, 2015.

Childers, Jay P. *The Evolving Citizen: American Youth and the Changing Norms of Democratic Engagement.* University Park: Pennsylvania State University Press, 2012.

Chowdhury, Elora Halim. *Transnationalism Reversed: Women Organizing Against Violence in Bangladesh.* Albany: SUNY, 2011.

Cisneros, David Josue. *The Border Crossed Us: Rhetorics of Borders, Citizenship, and Latin/o Identity.* Tuscaloosa: University of Alabama Press, 2013.

Clark, Gracia. *Onions Are My Husband: Survival and Accumulation by West African Market Women.* Chicago: University of Chicago Press, 1994.

Clifford, James. *Routes: Travel and Translation in the Late Twentieth Century.* Cambridge: Harvard University Press, 1997.

———. "Traveling Cultures." In *Cultural Studies,* edited by Lawrence Grossberg, Cary Nelson, and Paula Treichler, 96–116. New York: Routledge, 1992.

Collins, Patricia Hill. *Black Feminist Thought: Knowledge, Consciousness, and the Politics of Empowerment.* 2nd ed. New York: Routledge, 2000.

Condit, Celeste Michelle. *Decoding Abortion Rhetoric: Communicating Social Change.* Urbana: University of Illinois, 1990.

———. "The Functions of Epideictic: The Boston Massacre Orations as Exemplar." *Communication Quarterly* 33, no. 4 (1985): 284–98.

———. "Post-Burke: Transcending the Sub-Stance of Dramatism." *Quarterly Journal of Speech* 78, no. 3 (1992): 349–55.

Cooke, Miriam. *Women and the War Story.* Berkeley: University of California Press, 1996.

Cooper, Dana, and Claire Phelan, eds. *Motherhood and War: International Perspectives.* New York: Palgrave Macmillan, 2014.

Cooper, Helene. *Madame President: The Extraordinary Journey of Ellen Johnson Sirleaf.* New York: Simon and Schuster, 2017.

Daniels, Alfonso. "From Torture Victim to President." *Progressive* 70, no. 3 (2006): 30–32.

DeChaine, Robert. Afterword to *The Rhetorics of US Immigration: Identity, Community, Otherness,* edited by E. Johanna Artelius, 275–88. University Park: Pennsylvania State University Press, 2015.

———. *Global Humanitarianism: NGOs and the Crafting of Community.* Lanham: Lexington Books, 2005.

Delanty, Gerard. *Citizenship in a Global Age: Society, Culture, Politics.* Buckingham, UK: Open University Press, 2000.

DeLuca, Kevin Michael. *Image Politics: The New Rhetoric of Environmental Activism.* New York: Routledge, 1999.

Dennis, Benjamin G., and Anita K. Dennis. *Slaves to Racism: An Unbroken Chain from America to Liberia.* New York: Algora, 2008.

Denov, Myriam. *Child Soldiers: Sierra Leone's Revolutionary Front.* New York: Cambridge University Press, 2010.

Dingo, Rebecca. *Networking Arguments: Rhetoric, Transnational Feminism, and Public Policy Writing*. Pittsburgh: University of Pittsburgh Press, 2012.

Dingo, Rebecca, and J. Blake Scott, eds. *The Megarhetorics of Global Development*. Pittsburgh: University of Pittsburgh Press, 2012.

Dobrowolsky, Alexandra, and Evangelia Tastsoglou. "Crossing Boundaries and Making Connections." In *Women, Migration, and Citizenship: Making Local, National, and Transnational Connections,* edited by Evangelia Tastsoglou and Alexandra Dobrowolsky, 1–36. Burlington, VT: Ashgate, 2006.

Dow, Bonnie J. "Feminism and Public Address Research: Television News and the Constitution of Women's Liberation." In *The Handbook of Rhetoric and Public Address*, edited by Shawn J. Parry-Giles and J. Michael Hogan, 345–72. Malden, Mass.: Wiley-Blackwell, 2010.

Dow, Bonnie J., and Mari Boor Tonn. "'Feminine Style' and Political Judgment in the Rhetoric of Ann Richards." *Quarterly Journal of Speech* 79 (1993): 286–303.

Ekeh, Peter P. "Kinship and State in African and African American Histories." In *The African Diaspora: African Origins and New World Identities*, edited by Isidore Okpewho, Carole Boyce Davies, and Ali Al'Amin Mazrui, 89–114. Bloomington: Indiana University Press, 1999.

Falkner, Robert, Hannes Stephan, and John Vogler. "International Climate Policy after Copenhagen: Toward a 'Building Blocks' Approach." *Global Policy* 3 (2010): 252–62.

Felman, Shoshana, and Dori Laub. *Testimony: Crises of Witnessing in Literature, Psychoanalysis, and History*. New York: Routledge, 1992.

Ferree, Myra Marx. "Globalization and Feminism: Opportunities and Obstacles for Activism in the Global Arena." In *Global Feminism: Transnational Women's Activism, Organizing, and Human Rights*, edited by Myra Marx Ferree and Aili Mari Tripp, 3–23. New York: New York University Press, 2006.

Ferree, Myra Marx, and Aili Mari Tripp. Preface to *Global Feminism: Transnational Women's Activism, Organizing, and Human Rights*, edited by Myra Marx Ferree and Aili Mari Tripp, vii–ix. New York: New York University Press, 2006.

Ford, Tamasin. "Domestic Violence Is Biggest Threat to West Africa's Women, IRC Says." *Guardian*, May 22, 2012. https://www.theguardian.com/global-development/2012/may/22/domestic-violence-west-africa-irc.

———. "Wronged Women of Liberia Reluctant to Revisit Human Rights Abuses," *Guardian*, February 28, 2012.

Foss, Sonja K., and Cindy L. Griffin. "A Feminist Perspective on Rhetorical Theory: Toward a Clarification of Boundaries." *Western Journal of Communication* 56, no. 4 (1992): 330–49.

Franceschet, Susan. "Continuity or Change?: Gender Policy in the Bachelet Administration." In *The Bachelet Government: Conflict and Consensus in Post-Pinochet Chile*, edited by Silvia Borzutzy and Gregory B. Weeks, 158–80. Gainesville: University Press of Florida, 2010.

Franklin, James C. "Shame on You: The Impact of Human Rights Criticism on Political Repression in Latin America." *International Studies Quarterly* 52, no. 1 (2008): 187–211.

Fuest, Veronica. "'This Is the Time to Get out in Front': Changing Roles and Opportunities for Women in Liberia." *African Affairs* 107, no. 427 (2008): 201–22.

Gberie, Lansana. *A Dirty War in West Africa: The RUF and the Destruction of Sierra Leone*. Bloomington: Indiana University Press, 2005.

Gbowee, Leymah, and Carol Mithers. *Mighty Be Our Powers: How Sisterhood, Prayer, and Sex Changed a Nation at War*. New York: Beast Books, 2011.

Givoni, Michal. *The Care of the Witness: A Contemporary History of Testimony in Crises.* Cambridge: Cambridge University Press, 2016.

Glenn, Cheryl. *Rhetoric Retold: Regendering the Tradition from Antiquity through the Renaissance.* Carbondale: Southern Illinois University Press, 1997.

Grewal, Inderpal. *Transnational America: Feminisms, Diasporas, Neoliberalisms.* Durham: Duke University Press, 2005.

———. "'Women's Rights as Human Rights': Feminist Practices, Global Feminism, and Human Rights Regimes in Transnationality." *Citizenship Studies* 3, no. 3 (1999): 337–54.

Grewal, Inderpal, and Caren Kaplan. "Introduction: Transnational Feminist Practices and Questions of Postmodernity." In *Scattered Hegemonies: Postmodernity and Transnational Feminist Practices,* edited by Inderpal Grewal and Caren Kaplan, 1–33. Minneapolis: University of Minnesota Press, 1994.

Gutman, Amy. "Democratic Citizenship." In *For Love of Country: Debating the Limits of Patriotism,* edited by Joshua Cohen, 66–71. Boston: Beacon Press, 1996.

Haddad, Emily A., and William E. Schweinle. "The Feminine Political Persona: Queen Victoria, Ellen Johnson Sirleaf, and Michelle Bachelet." In *Women and Management: Global Issues and Promising Solutions,* edited by Michele A. Paludi, 309–22. Santa Barbara, CA: Praeger, 2013.

Hafner-Burton, Emilie M. "Sticks and Stones: Naming and Shaming the Human Rights Enforcement Problem." *International Organization* 62, no. 4 (2008): 689–716.

Hammar, Thomas. *Democracy and the Nation State: Aliens, Denizens, and Citizens in a World of International Migration.* Aldershot: Avesbury, 1990.

Haraway, Donna. *Simians, Cyborgs, and Women: The Reinvention of Nature.* New York: Routledge, 1991.

Harding, Sandra. *Whose Science? Whose Knowledge?: Thinking from Women's Lives.* Ithaca: Cornell University Press, 1991.

Harris, David. *Civil War and Democracy in West Africa: Conflict Resolution, Elections, and Justice in Sierra Leone and Liberia.* London: I. B. Tauris, 2011.

Hawhee, Debra. *Moving Bodies: Kenneth Burke at the Edges of Language.* Columbia: University of South Carolina Press, 1993.

Hayner, Priscilla. "Negotiating Peace in Liberia: Preserving the Possibility for Justice." Henry Dunant Centre for Humanitarian Dialogue, November 2007.

Heidegger, Martin. "Building Dwelling Thinking." In *Philosophy and the City: Classic to Contemporary Writings,* edited by Sharon M. Meagher, 119–24. New York: SUNY Press, 2008.

Heitlinger, Alena. "Émigré Feminism: An Introduction." In *Émigré Feminism: Transnational Perspectives,* edited by Alena Heitlinger, 3–16. Toronto: University of Toronto Press, 1999.

Hesford, Wendy S. "Global Turns and Cautions in Rhetoric and Composition Studies." *Publications of the Modern Language Association of America* 121, no. 3 (2006): 787–801.

Hesford, Wendy S., and Eileen E. Schell. "Configurations of Transnationality: Locating Feminist Rhetorics." *College English* 70, no. 5 (2008): 461–70.

Heuer, Jennifer Ngair. *The Family and the Nation: Gender and Citizenship in Revolutionary France, 1789–1830.* Ithaca: Cornell University Press, 2005.

Hoffman, Danny. *The War Machine: Young Men and Violence in Sierra Leone and Liberia.* Durham: Duke University Press, 2011.

Human Rights Watch. "How to Fight, How to Kill: Child Soldiers in Liberia." *Human Rights Watch* 16, no. 2 (A) (2004): 1. Retrieved from http://www.hrw.org/en/reports/2004/02/02/how-fight-how-kill.

———. "'We'll Kill You if You Cry'": Sexual Violence in the Sierra Leone Conflict." *Human Rights Watch* 15, no. 1 (A) (2003). Retrieved from https://www.hrw.org /report/2003/01/16/well-kill-you-if-you-cry/sexual-violence-sierra-leone-conflict.

Hutchings, Kimberly, and Roland Dannreuther, eds. *Cosmopolitan Citizenship*. New York: MacMillan Press, 1999.

Hyde, Michael J. *The Ethos of Rhetoric*. Columbia: University of South Carolina Press, 2004.

Ingram, James D. *Radical Cosmopolitics: The Ethics and Politics of Democratic Universalism*. New York: Columbia University Press, 2013.

Isocrates. *Isocrates*. Vol. 1. Edited by George Norlin. New York: G. P. Putnam's Sons, 1928.

Jarratt, Susan, and Lynn Worsham, eds. *Feminism and Composition Studies: In Other Words*. New York: Modern Language Association, 1998.

Jorgensen-Earp, Cheryl. *"The Transfiguring Sword": The Just War of the Women's Social and Political Union*. Tuscaloosa: University of Alabama Press, 1997.

Keck, Margaret E., and Kathryn Sikkink. *Activists Beyond Borders: Advocacy Networks in International Politics*. Ithaca: Cornell University Press, 1998.

Kells, Michelle Hall. *Héctor P. Garcia: Everyday Rhetoric and Mexican American Civil Rights*. Carbondale: Southern Illinois University Press, 2006.

Khagram, Sanjeev, James V. Riker, and Kathryn Sikkink, eds. *Restructuring World Politics: Transnational Social Movements, Networks, and Norms*. Minneapolis: University of Minnesota Press, 2002.

Komine, Ayako. "When Migrants Become Denizens: Understanding Japan as a Reactive Immigration Country." *Contemporary Japan* 26, no. 2 (2014): 197–222.

Kraut, Richard. *Aristotle: Political Philosophy*. Oxford: Oxford University Press, 2002.

Lacey, Kate. *Listening Publics: The Politics and Experience of Listening in the Media Age*. Cambridge: Polity Press, 2013.

Lakoff, George. *Communicating Our American Values and Vision*. New York: Farrar, Strauss and Giroux, 2006.

———. *Moral Politics: How Liberals and Conservatives Think*. Chicago: University of Chicago Press, 1996.

Lebovic, James H., and Eric Voeten. "The Politics of Shame: The Condemnation of Country Human Rights Practices in the UNHCR." *International Studies Quarterly* 50, no. 4 (2006): 861–88.

Leff, Michael. "Things Made by Words: Reflections on Textual Criticism." *Quarterly Journal of Speech* 78, no. 2 (1990): 223–31.

Lemmon, Gayle Tzemach. "Michelle Bachelet Has a Mission to Help the World's Women." *Newsweek*, September 12, 2011.

Levitt, Peggy. "Constructing Gender Across Borders: A Transnational Approach." In *Analyzing Gender, Intersectionality, and Multiple Inequalities: Global, Transnational, and Local Contexts*, edited by Esther Ngan-Ling Chow, Marcia Texler Segal, and Lin Tan, 163–84. Bingley, UK: Emerald, 2011.

Liebenow, J. Gus. *Liberia: The Quest for Democracy*. Bloomington: Indiana University Press, 1987.

Logan, Shirley Wilson. *"We Are Coming": The Persuasive Discourse of Nineteenth-Century Black Women*. Carbondale: Southern Illinois University Press, 1999.

———. *With Pen and Voice: A Critical Anthology of Nineteenth-Century African-American Women*. Carbondale: Southern Illinois University Press, 1995.

Lopéz, Daniel, and Tomás Sánchez-Criado. "Dwelling the Telecare Home Place, Location and Habitability." *Space and Culture* 12, no. 3 (2009): 343–58.

Lury, Celia. "The Objects of Travel." In *Touring Cultures: Transformations of Travel and Theory*, edited by Chris Rojek and John Urry, 75–95. London: Routledge, 1997.

Lyon, Arabella. *Deliberative Acts: Democracy, Rhetoric, and Rights*. University Park: Pennsylvania State University Press, 2013.

Lyon, Arabella, and Lester C. Olson. "Human Rights Rhetoric: Traditions of Testifying and Witnessing." *Rhetoric Society Quarterly* 41, no. 3 (2011): 203–12.

MacKenzie, Megan H. *Female Soldiers in Sierra Leone: Sex, Security, and Post-Conflict Development*. New York: New York University Press, 2012.

Mao, LuMing. "The Rhetoric of Responsibility: Practicing the Art of Recontextualization." *Rhetoric Review* 30, no. 2 (2011): 119–20, 131–32.

Marback, Richard. *Managing Vulnerability: South Africa's Struggle for Democratic Rhetoric*. Columbia: University of South Carolina Press, 2012.

Martin, Biddy, and Chandra T. Mohanty. "Feminist Politics: What's Home Got to Do with It?" In *Feminist Studies, Critical Studies*, edited by Teresa de Lauretis, 191–212. Bloomington: Indiana University Press, 1986.

McGee, Michael C. "In Search of 'The People': A Rhetorical Alternative." *Quarterly Journal of Speech* 61, no. 3 (1975): 235–49.

———. "Text, Context, and the Fragmentation of Culture." *Western Journal of Speech Communication* 54, no. 3 (1990): 274–89.

McGrew, Anthony G., and Paul G. Lewis, eds. *Global Politics: Globalization and the Nation State*. Cambridge: Polity Press, 1992.

McIntosh, Toga Gayewea (principal author). "Mobilizing Capacity for Reconstruction and Development." *National Human Development Report: Liberia 2006*. Monrovia, Liberia: United Nations Development Programme. http://hdr.undp.org/en/reports/national/africa/liberia/LIBERIA_2006_en.pdf.

McKee, Emily. *Dwelling in Conflict: Negev Landscapes and the Boundaries of Belonging*. Stanford: Stanford University Press, 2016.

McKinnon, Sara L. "(In)Hospitable Publics: Theorizing Modalities of Access to US Publics." In *Public Modalities: Rhetoric, Culture, Media, and the Shape of Public Life*, edited by Daniel C. Brower and Robert C. Asen, 131–53. Tuscaloosa: University of Alabama Press, 2010.

———. "Positioned in/by the State: Incorporation, Exclusion, and Appropriation of Women's Gender-Based Claims to Political Asylum in the United States." *Quarterly Journal of Speech* 97, no. 2 (2011): 178–200.

Moran, Mary H. *Civilized Women: Gender and Prestige in Southeastern Liberia*. Ithaca: Cornell University Press, 1990.

———. *Liberia: The Violence of Democracy*. Philadelphia: University of Pennsylvania Press, 2006.

———. "Our Mothers Have Spoken: Synthesizing Old and New Forms of Women's Political Authority in Liberia." *Journal of International Women's Studies* 13, no. 4 (2012): 51–66.

Moran, Mary, and M. Anne Pitcher. "The 'Basket Case' and the 'Poster Child': Explaining the End of Civil Conflicts in Liberia and Mozambique." *Third World Quarterly* 25, no. 3 (2004): 501–19.

Musolff, Andreas. *Political Metaphor Analysis: Discourse and Scenarios*. London: Bloomsbury, 2016.

Nagar, Richa, and Amanda Lock Swarr. "Introduction: Theorizing Transnational Feminist Praxis." In *Critical Transnational Feminist Praxis*, edited by Amanda Lock Swarr and Richa Nagar, 1–22. Albany: SUNY Press, 2010.

Naples, Nancy A. "The Challenges and Possibilities of Transnational Feminist Praxis." In *Women's Activism and Globalization: Linking Local Struggles and Transnational Politics*, edited by Nancy A. Naples and Manisha Desai, 267–82. New York: Routledge, 2002.

Naples, Nancy A., and Manisha Desai. Preface to *Women's Activism and Globalization: Linking Local Struggles and Transnational Politics*, edited by Nancy Naples and Manisha Desai, vii–viii. New York: Routledge, 2002.

———, eds. *Women's Activism and Globalization: Linking Local Struggles and Transnational Politics*. New York: Routledge, 2002.

Nussbaum, Martha C. "Patriotism and Cosmopolitanism." In *For Love of Country: Debating the Limits of Patriotism*, edited by Joshua Cohen, 3–20. Boston: Beacon Press, 1996.

———. "Toward a Globally Sensitive Patriotism." *Daedalus* 137, no. 3 (2008): 78–93.

Omanyondo, Marie-Claire O. "Sexual and Gender-Based Violence and Health Facility Needs Assessment: Liberia." World Health Organization, September 6, 2004, 17–18.

Omeje, Kenneth C. "Introduction: Discourses of the Liberian Civil War and the Imperatives of Peacebuilding." In *War to Peace Transition: Conflict Intervention and Peacebuilding in Liberia*, edited by Kenneth C. Omeje, 3–18. Lanham: University Press of America, 2009.

Ong, Aihwa. *Flexible Citizenship: The Cultural Logics of Transnationality*. Durham: Duke University Press, 1999.

Oyewumi, Oyeronke. "Abiyamo: Theorizing African Motherhood." *Jenda: A Journal of Culture and African Women Studies* 4, no. 1 (2003). http://www.jendajournal.com/.

———. "Family Bonds/Conceptual Binds: African Notes on Feminist Epistemologies." *Signs* 25, no. 4 (2000): 1093–98.

Palczewski, Catherine Helen. "Survivor Testimony in the Pornography Industry: Assessing Credibility in the Minneapolis Hearings and the Attorney General's Report." In *Warranting Assent: Case Studies in Argument Evaluation*, edited by Edward Schiappa, 257–81. Albany: SUNY Press, 1995.

Pauley, Garth E. *LBJ's American Promise: The 1965 Voting Rights Address*. College Station: Texas A&M University Press, 2007.

Peabody, Stanton. "Women Who Made a Difference." *Liberian Studies Journal* 31, no. 1 (2006): 63–89.

Perelman, Chaïm, and L. Olbrechts-Tyteca. *The New Rhetoric: A Treatise on Argumentation*. Translated by John Wilkinson and Purcell Weaver. Notre Dame: University of Notre Dame Press, 1969.

Phelps, Louise Wetherbee, and Janet Emig, eds. *Feminine Principles and Women's Experiences in American Composition and Rhetoric*. Pittsburgh: University of Pittsburgh Press, 1995.

Pickering, Barbara A. "Women's Voices as Evidence: Personal Testimony in Pro-choice Films." *Argumentation and Advocacy* 40 (2003): 1–22.

Pies, Ingo, and Peter Koslowski, eds. *Corporate Citizenship and New Governance: The Political Role of Corporations*. London: Springer, 2011.

Post, Robert. Introduction to *Another Cosmopolitanism*, by Seyla Benhabib, 1–9. Oxford: Oxford University Press, 2006.

Prasch, Allison. "Maternal Bodies in Militant Protest: Leymah Gbowee and the Rhetorical Agency of African Motherhood." *Women's Studies in Communication* 38, no. 2 (2015): 187–205.

Pratt, Mary Louise. *Imperial Eyes: Travel Writing and Transculturation*. New York: Routledge, 1992.

Railey, Doris H. "Some Impacts of the Liberian Civil War: A Pilot Study of Thirty Liberian Immigrant Families in the United States." *Liberian Studies Journal* 22, no. 2 (1997): 261–67.

Ramaswamy, Sumathi. *The Goddess and the Nation: Mapping Mother India*. Durham: Duke University Press, 2010.

Ranchod-Nilsson, Sita, and Mary Ann Tréreault, eds. *Women, States, and Nationalism: At Home in the Nation?* London: Routledge, 2000.

Ratcliffe, Krista. *Rhetorical Listening: Identification, Gender, Whiteness.* Carbondale: Southern Illinois University Press, 2005.

Reynolds, Nedra. *Geographies of Writing: Inhabiting Places and Encountering Difference.* Carbondale: Southern Illinois University Press, 2004.

Richards, Rebecca S. *Transnational Feminist Rhetorics and Gendered Leadership in Global Politics: From Daughters of Destiny to Iron Ladies.* Lanham: Lexington Books, 2015.

Rickert, Thomas. *Ambient Rhetoric: The Attunements of Rhetorical Being.* Pittsburgh: University of Pittsburgh Press, 2013.

Roberts, Kathleen Glenister. "Dialog Ethics, Cosmopolitanism, and Intercultural Communication." In *Communication Ethics: Between Cosmopolitanism and Provinciality*, edited by Kathleen Glenister Roberts and Ronald C. Arnett, 89–104. New York: Peter Lang, 2008.

Rosbrook-Thompson, James. "'I'm Local and Foreign': Belonging, the City, and the Case for Denizenship." *Urban Studies* 52, no. 9 (2015): 1615–30.

Rosenau, James N. "Emergent Spaces, New Places, Old Faces: Proliferating Identities in a Globalizing World." In *Worlds on the Move: Globalization, Migration, and Cultural Security*, edited by Jonathan Friedman and Shalini Randeria, 23–62. London: I. B. Tauris, 2004.

Rowe, Aimee Carillo. "Be Longing: Toward a Feminist Politics of Relation." *National Women's Studies Association Journal* 17, no. 2 (2005): 15–46.

———. "Whose 'America'?: The Politics of Rhetoric and Space in the Formation of U.S. Nationalism." *Radical History Review* 89 (2004): 115–34.

Royster, Jacqueline Jones, and Gesa E. Kirsch. *Feminist Rhetorical Practices: New Horizons for Rhetoric, Composition, and Literacy Studies.* Carbondale: Southern Illinois Press, 2012.

Runyan, Anne Sisson. "Global Feminism." In *Feminism and Women's Rights Worldwide*, edited by Michele A. Paludi, 1–16. Santa Barbara, CA: Praeger, 2010.

Schattle, Hans. *The Practices of Global Citizenship.* Lanham: Rowman and Littlefield, 2008.

Scott, Duncan. "Negotiated Denizenship: Foreign Nationals' Tactics of Belonging in a Cape Town Township." *Social Dynamics: A Journal of The Centre For African Studies University of Cape Town* 39, no. 3 (2013): 520–35.

Segal, Marcia Texler, and Esther Ngan-ling Chow. "Analyzing Gender, Intersectionality, and Inequality in Global, Transnational, and Local Contexts." In *Analyzing Gender, Intersectionality, and Multiple Inequalities: Global, Transnational, and Local Contexts*, edited by Esther Ngan-Ling Chow, Marcia Texler Segal, and Lin Tan, 1–16. Bingley, UK: Emerald, 2011.

Shearing, C., and J. Wood. "Nodal Governance, Democracy, and the New 'Denizens.'" *Journal of Law and Society* 30, no. 3 (2003): 400–419.

Sheeler, Kristina Horn, and Karrin Vasby Anderson. "Gender, Rhetoric, and International Political Systems: Angela Merkel's Negotiation of Proportional Representation and Party Politics." *Communication Quarterly* 62, no. 4 (2014): 474–95.

Shome, Raka. "Transnational Feminism and Communication Studies." *Communication Review* 9, no. 4 (2006): 255–67.

Sirleaf, Ellen Johnson. *This Child Will Be Great: Memoir of a Remarkable Life by Africa's First Woman President.* New York: HarperCollins, 2009.

Smith, Jackie, Charles Chatfield, and Ron Pagnucco, eds. *Transnational Social Movements and Global Politics: Solidarity Beyond the State.* Syracuse: Syracuse University Press, 1997.

Somini, Sengupta. "In the Mud, Liberia's Gentlest Rebels Pray for Peace." *New York Times*, July 1, 2003, 50.

Spivak, Gayatri. "Can the Subaltern Speak? Speculations on Widow Sacrifice." *Wedge* 7–8 (Winter–Spring 1985): 120–30.

Stiglitz, Joseph E. *Globalization and Its Discontents*. New York: W. W. Norton, 2002.

Stillion Southard, Belinda A. *Militant Citizenship: Rhetorical Strategies of the National Woman's Party, 1913–1920*. College Station: Texas A&M University Press, 2011.

Stirling, Kirsten. *Bella Caledonia: Woman, Nation, Text*. New York: Rodopi, 2008.

"Tackling Liberia's High Rape Rate." *IRIN News*, July 18, 2014, http://www.irinnews.org /report/100364/tackling-liberia's-high-rape-rate.

Tan, Kathy-Ann. *Reconfiguring Citizenship and National Identity in the North American Literary Imagination*. Detroit: Wayne State University Press, 2015.

Theobald, Anne. *The Role of Women in Making and Building Peace in Liberia: Gender Sensitivity versus Masculinity*. Stuttgart, Germany: ibidem-Verlag, 2013.

Thomas, Gwynn. "Bachelet's Liderazgo Femenino (Feminine Leadership)." *International Feminist Journal of Politics* 13, no. 1 (2011): 63–82.

Thomas, Gwynn, and Melinda Adams. "Breaking the Final Glass Ceiling: The Influence of Gender in the Elections of Ellen Johnson Sirleaf and Michelle Bachelet." *Journal of Women, Politics, and Policy* 31, no. 2 (2010): 105–31.

Tripp, Aili Mari. "The Evolution of Transnational Feminisms: Consensus, Conflict, and New Dynamics." In *Global Feminism*, edited by Myra Marx Ferree and Aili Mari Tripp, 51–75. New York: New York University Press, 2006.

Trofimov, Yaroslav. "In Liberia's War, Woman Commanded Fear and Followers." *Wall Street Journal—Eastern Edition*, August 22, 2003, A1–A2.

Vatz, Richard E. "The Myth of the Rhetorical Situation." *Philosophy and Rhetoric* 6, no. 3 (1973): 154–61.

Vieten, Ulrike M. *Gender and Cosmopolitanism in Europe: A Feminist Perspective*. Surrey, UK: Ashgate, 2012.

Walker, Neil. "Denizenship and the Deterritorialization in the EU." In *A Right to Inclusion and Exclusion?: Normative Fault Lines of the EU's Area of Freedom Security and Justice*, edited by Hans Lindahl, 261–72. Oxford: Hart, 2009.

Wanzer-Serrano, Darrel. *The New York Young Lords and the Struggle for Liberation*. Philadelphia: Temple University Press, 2015.

Wardhaugh, Julia. "The Unaccommodated Woman: Home, Homelessness, and Identity." *Sociological Review* 47, no. 1 (1999): 91–109.

Weiss, Thomas G., and Ramesh Shakur. *Global Governance and the UN: An Unfinished Journey*. Bloomington: Indiana University Press, 2010.

Werbner, Pnina. "Introduction: Towards a New Cosmopolitan Anthropology." In *Anthropology and the New Cosmopolitanism: Rooted, Feminist, and Vernacular Perspectives*, edited by Pnina Werbner, 1–32. Oxford: Berg, 2008.

West, Isaac. *Transforming Citizenships: Transgender Articulations of the Law*. New York: New York University Press, 2014.

Wilson, Kirt H. *The Reconstruction Desegregation Debate: The Politics of Equality and the Rhetoric of Place, 1870–1875*. East Lansing: Michigan State University Press, 2002.

Woodhull, Winnie. "Global Feminisms, Transnational Political Economies, Third World Cultural Production." *Journal of International Women's Studies* 4, no. 2 (2003): 76–90.

Zaeske, Susan. *Signatures of Citizenship: Petitioning, Antislavery, and Women's Political Identity*. Chapel Hill: University of North Carolina Press, 2003.

INDEX

RHETORIC AND **DEMOCRATIC** DELIBERATION

Typeset by
BOOKCOMP, INC.

Printed and bound by
SHERIDAN BOOKS

Composed in
SCALA

Printed on
NATURES NATURAL